Queerbook

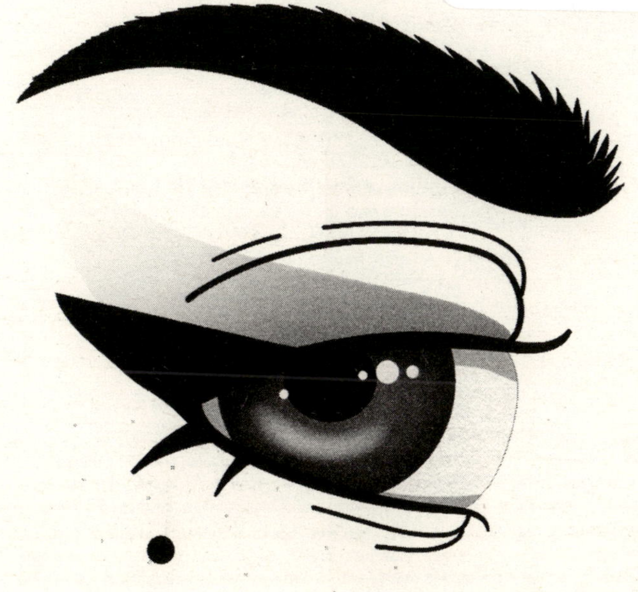

For the brilliant weirdos who choose authenticity with the prospect of rejection and ridicule rather than live 'a sick and boring life'. And the faithful pup, the pickle and the bear for getting me here. – M.M.

For all the queer people who came before me, the amazing queer community in Norwich and of course my wonderful Angie who I would be lost without. – E.F.

First published in Great Britain 2024 by Red Shed, part of Farshore
An imprint of HarperCollins*Publishers*
1 London Bridge Street, London SE1 9GF
www.farshore.co.uk

HarperCollins*Publishers*
Macken House, 39/40 Mayor Street Upper, Dublin 1, D01 C9W8

Illustrated by Emily A. Foster
Cover illustration by Madelen Foss

Consultancy by Gabriel Duckels and Dr Patricia Macnair

ISBN 978 0 00 863714 9
Printed in the UK.
001

A CIP catalogue record for this title is available from the British Library.

This book makes reference to individuals whom we believe are important to an understanding of LGBTQ+ history and culture. A mention in this book does not represent an endorsement of an individual's views. This book also contains some references to sex and violence.

This book contains FSC™ certified paper and other controlled sources to ensure responsible forest management.

For more information visit: www.harpercollins.co.uk/green

Queerbook

Malcolm Mackenzie

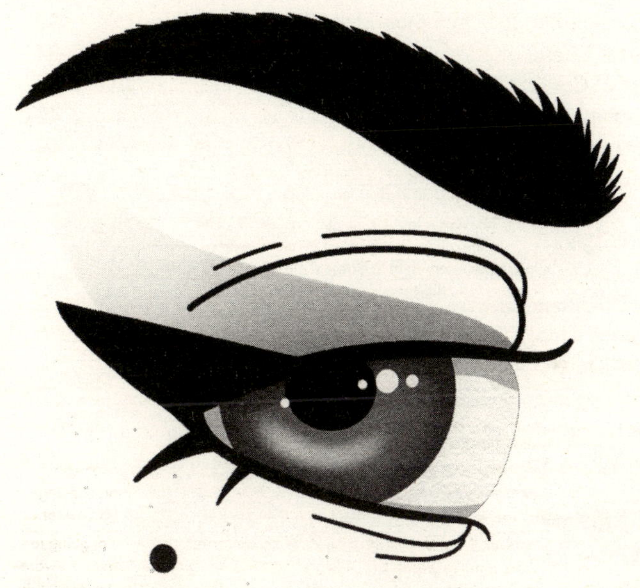

Contents

Queered-up Culture

We have chosen to use LGBTQ+ in this book, rather than any of the other widely used acronyms to describe sexual and gender identity minorities. At the time of printing, LGBTQ+ is the acronym most commonly used within the queer community itself (source: YouGov, 2023).

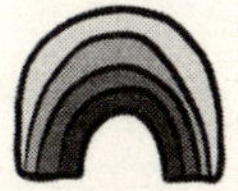

Introduction

Welcome to *Queerbook*! Phew, you made it! Get ready for a deep dive – a plunge, even – into LGBTQ+ fabulousness. Why is this book so special? Well . . .

Being LGBTQ+ comes with a rich cultural and social history, but unlike communities drip-fed their heritage through shared backgrounds and beliefs, ours remains largely hidden. Why? Because over the years, our identity has been mostly hidden too. Our homes are rarely filled with people like us. The majority of parents aren't queer, and heterosexuality is assumed. Which means we usually have to look beyond the family to understand who we are.

But – don't despair. Queerness is EVERYWHERE and it always has been. Just like we haven't all evolved to be tall, we will never all evolve to be straight. Sexuality and gender identity are a small but essential part of the variation that makes humans so successful.

There are stacks of incredible books that delve into specific nooks and crannies of queer culture, highlighting heroes of this, that, and, of course, the other. But *Queerbook* has all of it – everything, everyone, all at once. You don't need any specific interests to read it; all you need is curiosity and a desire to learn more about what it means to be LGBTQ+ (psst, allies, you're invited too. Queer history is world history; the more straight champions we have, the better). This whistlestop tour of WTF info is like pressing shuffle on all the fun queer stuff that you deserve to know but possibly don't: heroes and stories, art and science, facts and stats. It puts 'our story' back into history and will set you straight, *ahem*, on all the definitions and acronyms you've seen flying around but might not have pinned down.

I am not the reason this book is brilliant. The content speaks for itself. That said, here's a quick Wiki-style biog to give you an idea of where I'm coming from . . .

I grew up on the sunny British island of Jersey in the 1980s when being gay (and acting on it) was illegal for anyone of any age. The only time I heard about gay people was as a joke or a slur: "You want to be an actor? Watch out, they're all poofs." It didn't put me off doing the school panto.

Forming my own queer identity under these constraints was no easy task. I knew there had to be more to gay life, but with no internet (yes, really), I had to exercise cat-like vigilance to find any representation. Whenever the queer world slipped into my eyeline, I leapt up and pressed record on the TV, or ripped pages out of magazines and filed them for safe-keeping. Slowly I began accumulating a magical database of queerness. I still have some of my scrapbooks. This is what we do as LGBTQ+ people – in order to survive, we search for proof that others like us are out there living happy lives so we can dream of a future where we will flourish too.

Queerbook is an extension of my scrapbooks – a compilation of all the good queer intel that the foghorn of straight culture has drowned out. It's rose-coloured sunglasses onto a bright alternate queer reality, the choice to say 'no' to the Straightrix, to leave Kansas and enter the technicolour world over the rainbow.

Queer we go . . .

This Is Us

Got Your Number

We're here, we're queer – but how many of us are there, exactly?

When it comes to queer representation in the media, we're everywhere! That's how it seems at least. But what percentage of people do you think are LGBTQ+ in the UK? Go on, have a guess . . .

If you guessed **four per cent**, you'd be about right. But the truth is, it's incredibly hard to pin down exact figures. Surveys and studies are all well and good, but there are always people who aren't captured by the data. It's even harder to work out worldwide statistics, as there are countries where being LGBTQ+ is illegal and people actively hide their identity.

Censuses – questionnaires filled out by everyone in a country at a specific time – are helpful for getting some data. A census of people aged 16 and older is carried out every ten years in England and Wales to find out more about the population. Here are a couple of questions from the 2021 census:

Q: Which of the following best describes your sexual orientation?

43.4 million identified as straight

1.5 million were lesbian, gay or bisexual (3.2 per cent). (Of those, 748,000 said they were gay or lesbian, and 624,000 said they were bi)

112,00 were pansexual

28,000 were asexual

15,000 identified as queer

10,000 described their sexuality as something different

Q: Is the gender you identify with the same as your sex registered at birth?

45.4 million people answered 'yes'

262,000 people answered 'no' (0.5 per cent or 1 in 200 people)

118,000 said 'no' and gave no further information

48,000 identified as a trans man

48,000 identified as a trans woman

30,000 identified as non-binary

18,000 specified an alternative gender identity

This adds up to **3.7 per cent** – a whopping **1.76 million people** – identifying themselves as LGBTQ+. And remember, not everyone who identifies as LGBTQ+ would have felt comfortable answering the question. Censuses are given to households rather than individuals, so these questions are hard to answer for anyone not out to the people they live with. There were 3.6 million people who did not answer the sexuality question at all.

According to a 2022 Gallup poll in the US, and UK data from the Office for National Statistics, bisexual people make up a massive part of the community. This is particularly true for women, who tend to be more sexually fluid than men and three times more likely to be bisexual. In both the US and UK, the 'B' in LGBTQ+ makes up approximately half of us. What does that mean?

1. Don't assume all male-female couples are straight, or that all same-sex couples are gay or lesbian.
2. More bisexual representation in the media is essential.

Call Me By What Name?

The terminology for people who fall under the LGBTQ+ umbrella is constantly evolving. Chances are that this page is already outdated.

In the past, homosexuality was mostly something a person *did*, not something a person *was*. So, generally, words from the past meaning homosexual were used to describe people who were paid for gay sex (mostly as a slur). Many of these terms have now gone out of use, like 50 per cent of town-centre toilets. Others, however, are still going strong. Today, a whole host of words are used around the world to describe LGBTQ+ people, sexualities and genders. Here are a just few of them, along with an approximate date for their first recorded appearance. Some are popular, some outdated, some reclaimed, some downright offensive – you name it!

The Kinsey Scale

Thinking about sexuality definitions isn't a 21st century idea. In 1948, bisexual biologist and sexologist **Alfred Kinsey** released research showing that people don't fit into neat boxes of homosexual or heterosexual – his sliding scale of 0 (exclusively straight) to 6 (exclusively homosexual) completely changed how we think about sexuality.

Terms in use today

Ally (1990s) – A person who isn't part of the queer community but actively supports LGBTQ+ rights.

Asexual (1890s) – Not sexually attracted to anyone (or experiencing little sexual attraction).

Bisexual (1970s) – Attracted to both men and women. Before the word intersex was adopted, bisexuality was used to describe people with both male and female sex characteristics.

Butch (1940s) – Masculine-presenting lesbian, trans man or non-binary person.

Cisgender (1994) – This term was created by biologist Dana Deleland Defosse to give a name to people who identify with the sex they were given at birth. It really just means 'not trans'.

Demisexual (2006) – Demi means half. The term was originally conceived as a sort of halfway place between sexual and asexual. Today, it means those who only feel attracted to people they have an emotional relationship with.

Dyke (1920s) – Arising from the slang for vulva, this one-time insult has been reclaimed by some lesbians.

Gay (1930s) – Gay used to just mean happy, but in the 1930s, it took on a new additional meaning. This was the first word to describe queer people that didn't sound like a condemnation or diagnosis. The first use in popular culture came from Cary Grant in the 1938 film *Bringing Up Baby* – while jumping up and down in a woman's dressing gown.

Genderqueer (1990s) – Adopted around the same time as queer by those rejecting the binary of their assigned sex.

Heteroflexible (2000s) – Either a term to describe mostly-straight people who want to leave themselves open to the possibility of same-sex experiences, or a bogus term invented by people wanting to hold onto 'straight privilege'? You decide.

Homosexual (1890s) – A diagnostic term created by Austrian-Hungarian Károly Mária Kertbeny. He also invented the word heterosexual.

Lesbian (1730s) – Women who love women are said to come from Lesbos, a Greek island where the ancient poet Sappho lived. Somewhat poetic, when you think about it.

Non-binary (2000) – A general term for many identities that describes those of us who identify neither as male nor female but feel they either sit somewhere between the two or identify as a separate third gender.

Pansexual (1990s) – This super-inclusive sexuality comes from the ancient Greek 'pan', meaning 'all'. Generally speaking, pansexual people are attracted to people regardless of how they identify, be they male or female, non-binary, cis or trans.

Queer (1935) – Queer, meaning strange or odd, was originally used as an insult but has now been reclaimed by the LGBTQ+ community.

WSW/MSM (1990s) – Following the AIDS crisis of the 1980s, the terms WSW (women who have sex with women) and MSM (men who have sex with men) were introduced by health professionals to avoid the thorny issue of identity. When looking at sexual health, it's often what you do that counts not how you see yourself.

Outdated terms

Hermaphrodite (1400) – A portmanteau (combination of words) of the names Hermes and Aphrodite. According to mythology, these two Greek gods were the parents of Hermaphroditus, a beautiful male god who ended up being joined together with a female nymph, Salmacis. The word became synonymous with describing those with intersex traits, but is usually considered a slur today.

Macaroni (1770s) – Big-wigged hipsters of their day. 'Queer' as an identity, rather than an action, starts here.

Molly (1708) – Molly, a nickname for girls called Mary, was also used in Georgian times for flamboyant homosexuals in pouffy white wigs.

Pansy (1929) – Insulting gay men by naming them after a pretty little flower. How imaginative.

Sapphist (1890) – Sappho was a highly regarded ancient Greek female poet who celebrated love between women.

Sodomite (538BCE) – Sodom was a city mentioned in the Bible as being destroyed for its wickedness. According to one (homophobic) interpretation of the biblical text from the sixth century BCE (Hi, Emperor Justinian), a rowdy mob from Sodom were guilty of ravaging men by force – and so the term was born.

Tommy (1780) – Slang name given to women who loved women in the 18th century.

Of course, this list isn't exhaustive – you'll find many more terms as you go through this book, and new terms are being born all the time. Padam.

Biology Lesson

What makes us queer? Is it in our genes, in the way our body works, or is it something we pick up as we go through life?

There is no gay gene

Contrary to what many people believe, there is no single 'gay gene'. In fact, it's probably a small contribution from thousands rather than just one, as many genes influence human sexuality. But even then, you can't blame genes for everything – studies have shown that genetics account for only 8–25 per cent of what makes a person engage in same-sex sexual activity, and the most any single gene contributes is only about one per cent.

Hormonal AF

Hormones are well known to influence sexuality throughout life – and may even be important before we're born. Until the sixth week of pregnancy, an embryo is neither male nor female. It's only the production of male hormones that makes the embryo develop male internal and external genitalia – and the amount of male hormones an embryo receives *may* be a predictor of future same-sex desire. A study from 2000 found that lesbians and gay men may have been exposed to higher doses of testosterone in the womb. Fluctuations in exposure to testosterone *in utero* may also result in a person experiencing gender dysphoria and subsequently identifying as trans.

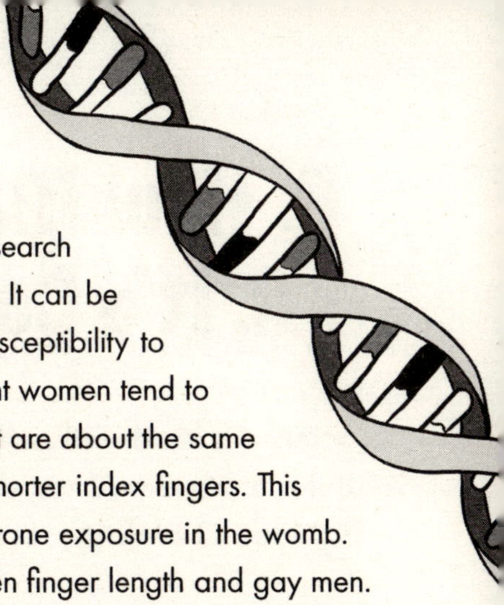

Size matters . . . finger size

A weirdly large amount of research has been done on finger length. It can be a predictor of eating habits, susceptibility to disease – and sexuality. Straight women tend to have index and ring fingers that are about the same length. Lesbians tend to have shorter index fingers. This may relate to pre-natal testosterone exposure in the womb. No link has been found between finger length and gay men. Research on finger length has caused heated debate though, with researchers arguing about how reliable the studies are.

We can smell sexuality – no, really!

We know that smell plays a part in animals' sexuality – and it does in humans too. A 2005 study discovered that gay men found the smell of sweat from other gay men and straight women most attractive. The noses of straight men, straight women and lesbians deemed the body odour of gay men least pleasing.

Is Darwin's paradox extinct?

According to Charles Darwin, species evolve to create future generations that are more likely to survive. But where do same-sex couples fit in? Scientists have been looking for a biological reason to explain homosexual behaviour for years. In the animal world, various theories have suggested that gay males aren't seen as a threat to the pack leader (as they don't compete for females), that bisexual behaviour is good for bonding, and that living in a more diverse group makes adaptation and survival more likely. It's not rocket science – apes get it; sadly bigots don't.

Q. How Many Sexes? A. It's Complicated

Science is hard – it's why we get scientists to do it. But to understand sex differences, we do need to look at biology, and specifically genetics.

Basic genetics

1. Most people have **46 chromosomes** in each cell of our body. These are packages of DNA that carry genetic information given to us by our mums and dads. Most chromosomes contain hundreds of individual genes.
2. We get **23 chromosomes** (half of our genetic information) from each of our parents.
3. The sex chromosomes **X and Y** determine which sex we are. The most common arrangement of these chromosomes are XX (female biological sex) and XY (male biological sex).
4. Except, it's not that simple . . .

Beyond XX and XY

Some people don't have the standard 46 chromosomes in all or some of their cells. This can have varying effects, some of which relate to whether the body develops in more or less typically male or female ways. The addition or absence of an X or Y chromosome can cause genetic conditions including:

45 chromosomes (X, sometimes described as XO) – Turner Syndrome

- **1 in about every 2,000 females.**
- It can result in individuals being smaller, having lower levels of the female hormone oestrogen, and not experiencing the sexual development associated with puberty.

47 chromosomes (XXY) – Klinefelter Syndrome

- **1 in 500–1,000 males** (as many as two thirds go undiagnosed).
- People with this condition are genetically male but with less pronounced masculine features and more female characteristics. They may be particularly tall with small and underactive testicles.

47 chromosomes (XYY) – Jacobs Syndrome

- **1 in 1,000 males.**
- People with this condition are usually taller and have an increased chance of mild learning difficulties (such as delayed development of speech, language and motor skills) and behavioural problems.
- Boys with Jacobs are more likely to have a very curved pinkie finger (called clinodactyly).

48 chromosomes (XXXY)

- **1 in 50,000 males.**
- Like Klinefelter Syndrome but much rarer. The addition of two extra X chromosomes can cause increased occurrence of feminising symptoms.

What does 'intersex' mean?

People with intersex traits exhibit variations of sexual characteristics that don't fit traditional ideas about how male and female bodies behave or look. These characteristics can be visible, such as external genital differences, or internal and invisible: hormones, chromosomes, gonads and reproductive organs. While many people use the term 'intersex' and add the 'I' to LGBTQIA+, not everyone likes it. The NHS refers to Differences in Sex Development (DSD), while others prefer Variations in Sex Characteristics (VSC). However, these medicalised terms are equally divisive. They may be helpful to identify the needs of a group, but we're people, not pathologies; ultimately, people can choose how they want to label themselves – if at all.

Gene teams

It's not all down to differences in whole chromosomes – there may be significant differences in just one or two of the genes within a single chromosome. Quite a few common genetic mutations can result in differences in sex characteristics. These include Congenital Adrenal Hyperplasia (CAH), which occurs in about **1 in 1,000** people when the adrenal gland produces excess male hormones, and Androgen Insensitivity Syndrome (AIS). People born with AIS have XY chromosomes so could be considered genetically male, but their bodies do not react to male hormones, so they don't develop in the same way as most males. This is known as 46, XY DSD: Androgen Insensitivity Syndrome and it affects up to about **1 in 20,000** people.

Sex as a spectrum

Textbook genetics states that biologically we're either male or female, but so many factors can contribute to male/female-ness that for some people, sex definitely lies on a spectrum. Randomness and mutation are a natural part of Life with a capital 'L'. If that wasn't the case, we wouldn't be capable of evolving, would we?

Lightbulb moment

Stats about the occurrence of intersex traits are as varied as the traits themselves. Estimates of those with some form of DSD range from **1.7 per cent** (a figure that has been challenged) to around **one in 1,000** (about 67,000 people in the UK). What we know for certain: society has made it incredibly difficult to opt out of the male-female binary. We have scientific proof that a significant proportion of the population has some form of DSD, yet everyone and their Uncle Bob has an argument ready to go on gender identification.

ASSUMPTION SMASH

Being intersex is something that needs to be fixed

We're so stuck on the male-female binary that often parents of a child with intersex traits feel compelled to make a choice for their child as soon as possible, but medical intervention isn't necessary for everyone. Whenever possible, the choice should come down to the individual when they're old enough to make the decision.

You Filthy Animal

'It's not natural!' is a phrase that every queer person has heard at some time or other. In actual fact, homosexual behaviour has been seen in over 1,500 species, making it pretty clear that nature does what it damn well pleases. What animals do NOT do, though, is judge others for their behaviour.

Penguins

In 1911, a zoologist on an Antarctic expedition recorded same-sex behaviour between male Adélie penguins, but the 'unsavoury' findings were not published until 2012. And Adélies aren't the only kind. Gay gentoo penguins Sphen and Magic from Sea Life in Sydney got together in 2018, and were so eager to become parents that they built their nest using more pebbles than the other penguin parents. Show-offs. It paid off handsomely when they welcomed their baby, called Sphengic!

Albatrosses

About 30 per cent of albatross pairs on the Hawaiian island of Oahu are females – making it possibly the greatest homosexual animal colony in the world. Albatrosses are monogamous, so two females might hook up for decades.

Sheep

Turns out sheep don't all follow the flock. In farming about eight per cent of male sheep exclusively get the horn for fellow rams.

Dolphins

Both male and female bottlenose dolphins show same-sex behaviour. In fact, some studies show that gay and straight sex is about equal in these clever cuties.

Lions

The 'king of the jungle' (OK, savanna . . .) is a bisexual king. Males regularly team up and hump each other, establishing dominance, reinforcing bonds and, by not killing each other, make sure their species thrives.

Giraffes

How's the air up there? Pretty gay. Up to a staggering 90 per cent of sexual activity between giraffes is same-sex. Male giraffes are all about necking – rubbing each other's necks against each other for up to an hour at a time.

Bonobos

One of our closest relations in the animal kingdom, bonobos are famously sex-positive, enjoying a smooch, and much more, with anyone in their troop. Male, female – it really doesn't matter.

Swans

Swans are so gay. Look at them. Up to one in four swans pairs up with an individual of the same sex. It's not all romance though: some males will mate with a female and once she's laid the eggs, tell her to 'flap off'.

Relationship Dictionary

Our emotional lives are more complicated than Star Wars LEGO®.

Romantic orientation

Romantic orientation describes the kind of person that you're romantically attracted to . . . who you might want to affectionately share blanket time with on a sofa while you binge hours of gaming walk-throughs. This is different from sexual orientation – for example, you might fancy someone but not want to get cosy with them. You might have heart-swelling feelings for someone but not want to snog the braces off them. Most people are attracted romantically and physically to the same people – but not everyone, asexual people in particular. Distinguishing between romantic attraction and sexual attraction makes it easier for these people to describe their feelings.

Here are some of the words people may use:

Aromantic – A person who doesn't really experience romantic attractions.

Biromantic – Having romantic attractions to men and women.

Heteroromantic – Someone who is romantically attracted only to people of the opposite sex.

Homoromantic – Those who are attracted to their own sex in a romantic way.

Panromantic – A romantic attraction to people regardless of gender.

Types of relationships

Romantic attraction is one thing. The relationships people get into is a whole other. Here are just a few types of relationship structure . . .

Consensual non-monogamy – CNM describes relationships that are considered 'open', for example having a main girlfriend but dating other people. It's different from cheating because it doesn't involve lying and gaslighting and being a complete douchebag.
Monogamy – Having a special relationship with one person, and one person alone. Not as sad as it sounds.
Polyamory – Having more than one ongoing relationship at the same time. Not as complicated as it sounds.
Thruple – Three people in a committed relationship with each other.
Unicorn – A situation where a single person dates couples. Insert joke about being horny.
Vee – A relationship where one person consensually and openly dates two people who aren't dating.

The most important word on this page is 'consensual'. Never be pressured and never put pressure on someone else. The saying 'try it, you might like it' is sometimes true, but nobody should try anything they don't want to. Trust your instincts. All relationships come with their ups and downs, some styles will have benefits that others do not. We all deserve to be loved, and it's worth trying to get the version of love that's right for us.

Intersectionality

The LGBTQ+ community doesn't only have to navigate prejudices such as homophobia, transphobia and misogyny (sometimes on a daily basis). There's a whole other bunch of factors too.

Intersectionality in a nutshell

Gay this, queer that, identity, sexuality . . . sometimes we're so focused on one part of ourselves that we neglect to take into account the others. The concept of intersectionality was developed by Kimberlé Crenshaw, a Black feminist scholar, in 1989. It's a view of identity that takes into consideration all the different facets of a person. Queer people share certain experiences but not all of them. I'm a gay, white, cis male. Today, that almost sounds like privilege. I almost certainly face fewer obstacles and hardships than many, because white people do not face the racism that people of colour experience, and cis people do not face the transphobia that the trans community are up against. Intersectionality hinges on your ability to move through the world with ease.

Intersectionality is part of all of our lives – and it can play out in all sorts of ways. A biggie is 'pretty privilege'. Being conventionally attractive gives people a leg up, because we're all so shallow that we usually treat hot people better. Weirdly though, if you're really hot, you can face a set of bonus complications, because we also tend to make assumptions about beautiful people, not all of them good.

Here are just a few examples of other factors that might come into play when considering your life as a queer person or ally:

age • caregiving responsibilities
colourism • cultural differences • dietary needs
disabilities • education • ethnicity
family support • gender expression • income
mental health issues • neurodiversity • outness
race • religious beliefs • size/weight
socio-economic background • transness
trauma experience

ASSUMPTION SMASH

Intersectional theory is a game of Top Trumps

No. The person with the most or fewest 'points of difference' isn't the winner. Thinking about, and being aware of, our differences is a tool to help us empathise with others' specific experiences, as well as reflecting and challenging the assumptions we make about the world based on our own experience.

Homophobia: The Dark Side of the Rainbow

Let's be honest, they're not scared, we are.

What is homophobia?

Homophobia, noun: hatred, dislike or prejudice against gay people or the LGBTQ+ community. The term was coined by (straight) psychotherapist George Weinberg in 1972. But homophobia didn't begin in the 1970s – it has a long history. From laws introduced hundreds of years ago to vile social media comments today, homophobia has existed in thousands of different forms. Sadly, incidents of homophobic abuse are still happening all over the world.

The confusion, mistrust, dislike – and, in some cases, even hatred – that our community sometimes faces can play out in hundreds of different ways. There are some types of homophobia that you might see every day, in the form of slurs, rude jokes or not including people because of their sexuality. Homophobia is so baked into our society that some people don't even realise they're being homophobic idiots. There are other types of homophobia that, with any luck, you will come across very seldom, or avoid altogether, such as assault. Some forms of homophobia can even work their way into law. For example, some US states have passed 'drag bans', making public drag performances illegal. Dumb, but also scary.

Homophobia in numbers and stats

1 in 8

The number of victims of homophobic hate crimes who actually report what happened to them.

32%

The year-on-year increase in homophobic hate crimes in the UK between 2021 and 2022, the biggest rise on record. An increase in homophobia – or people feeling more confident to report it? Or both?

70%

The percentage of trans people who report being impacted by transphobia when accessing general health services.

4,399

The number of transphobic hate crimes reported in the UK (2021–2022), a rise of 240 per cent in five years.

50%

Young LGBTQ+ people are more than 50 per cent more likely to experience online hate speech compared to those who see themselves as straight.

8%

The percentage of hate crimes against queer victims that result in prosecution.

Why are people homophobic?

Phobia literally means fear – fear is the root cause of all prejudice. When humans come across something different from themselves, or that they don't understand, they can react through attack, just like some animals. Homophobia is often a pack pursuit, something that the 'in-group' do to separate themselves from the 'out-group'. The fear in homophobia isn't that gay people are out having fun; it's that people might think that you're gay and persecute you. Or that your child will grow up to be gay, and people will ridicule you because of it. Ugh – so sad and selfish.

Homophobia isn't about us. It's really about other people struggling with their own desire to fit in and 'be normal' and be perceived as normal, as a way of asserting dominance and holding onto power. This plays out in all kinds of prejudice – racism, classism, sexism, religious discrimination, you name it. Prejudice is a biological throwback to protect our tribe and protect our own interests by ostracising others. Some of us humans like to think we're not total beasts though. We override narcissistic, irrational behaviour to try to make the world a better place. When we flourish physically and mentally, we're free to live our best lives and usually wish for others to do the same.

Homophobia as a political weapon

The terrifying thing is that homophobia doesn't just happen between individuals – it can happen for large-scale reasons. In the world of politics, attacking people is an easy form of control because it doesn't cost much and doesn't require you to do anything, which is why certain politicians are regularly vile to the LGBTQ+ community. Making the world a better place by paying a sensible wage for decent jobs and providing good homes and education costs a bomb – much easier to divert people with talk of willies and boobs and bums. After all, they *are* very diverting.

What can you do about it?

Homophobia is real, but the world is changing all the time, and the loudest voices aren't always majority voices. For every homophobic tool there will be a supportive, inclusive community – it's just a matter of finding them. There are plenty of things that we can do to look after ourselves and support each other, whether you're part of the community or not.

- Find your tribe – spending time with others who understand and celebrate you can be invaluable.
- Prioritise self-care – always ask for help if you need it. There are helplines and organisations dedicated to the LGBTQ+ community. Remember, it's OK to not always have the headspace to tackle homophobia head on.
- If you see someone receiving LGBTQ+ abuse, make them aware that you're there to help. It could mean helping them move away from the situation or reporting it. Make sure you don't put yourself in danger in the process.
- Make a habit of calling out your friends if they make homophobic jokes. The more they hear people resisting these jokes, the less normalised homophobic language becomes – a win all round.
- Check in with LGBTQ+ friends – if you're able, lend a listening ear if they're struggling.

Queer Liberation

It gets better, then it gets worse, then it gets better again. But throughout our history, people have been brave enough to take a stand . . .

1914

Edward Carpenter and Havelock Ellis found the British Society for the Study of Sex Psychology.

1908–1909

Sexologist Magnus Hirschfeld works with German police to issue 'transvestite passes', allowing people to dress in a manner opposite to their assigned birth-sex.

1908

Edward Carpenter's book *The Intermediate Sex* is published, offering a defence of same-sex love and gender non-conformity.

1919

Magnus Hirschfeld opens the Institute for Sexual Science in Berlin, studying all aspects of the LGBTQ+ experience.

1933

Nazis seize Magnus Hirschfeld's book archive and burn it. Hirschfield is abroad and does not return to his home country.

1948

The Kinsey Report on Male Sexuality is published, revealing the prevalence of same-sex behaviour for the first time.

1967

The Sexual Offences Act legalises private sexual acts between consenting males aged over 21 in England and Wales.

1966

The Beaumont Society, the longest-running UK trans support group, is set up.

1966

Following repeated abuses at the hands of police, over-it trans women and drag queens start the Compton's Cafeteria riot in San Francisco.

1553

The first anti-LGBTQ+ legislation, The Buggery Act, is introduced during the reign of Henry VIII. Sodomy is now punishable by death.

1785

English social reformer Jeremy Bentham argues that homosexuality is a victimless crime and not deserving of punishment.

1861

The death penalty for sodomy is removed but replaced with a minimum of ten years in prison.

1867

German lawyer Karl Heinrich Ulrichs becomes the first gay man to publicly 'come out' and demand rights for homosexuals.

1897

George Cecil Ives, a friend of Oscar Wilde, forms The Order of Chaeronea, a secret society that acts as a support group for 'the cause'.

1904

German journalist Anna Rüling, the first openly lesbian activist, gives a pioneering political speech shining a light on the problems faced by lesbians.

1950

In Los Angeles, Harry Hay, Chuck Rowland and Bob Hull form the gay social and activist group, The Mattachine Society.

1955

Lesbian activist group Daughters of Bilitis is created in San Francisco by four lesbian couples. Members include Rose Bamberger, Rosemary Sliepen, Phyllis Lyon and Del Martin.

1956

Black civil rights activist James Baldwin publishes the romantic gay novel *Giovanni's Room* – a ground-breaking political act in itself.

1957

The Wolfenden Report, commissioned by the UK government, is published – it recommends decriminalising gay sex.

1964

The Manchester-based Campaign for Homosexual Equality is founded by Labour councillor Allan Horsfall.

1964

The first protest for gay civil rights takes place in New York City.

1969

After systematic monthly raids, patrons of the Stonewall Inn, New York, fight back, resulting in the Stonewall Riots.

1970s

Zaps take place. Zaps are direct political actions intended to gain media coverage and make life difficult for outspoken homophobes.

1970

The Gay Liberation Front (GLF) is formed in the UK.

1987

Radical New York activist group ACT UP forms to protest the shocking lack of action in the US in the wake of the AIDS crisis.

1988

Section 28 is introduced in the UK, banning the 'promotion of homosexuality' in schools, in effect supressing LGBTQ+ identities.

1989

Stonewall, a UK queer support network and organisation for positive change, is founded.

1990

Activist group OutRage! is formed. One of their many protests is the Piccadilly Circus 'kiss-in', which arguably ended criminalisation of same-sex public displays of affection.

2003

Section 28 is finally repealed, removing it from UK law.

2004

The Civil Partnership Act allows same-sex couples in the UK to legally register their commitment to each other.

1971–1973

The Furies Collective forms in Washington DC, a commune comprised of 12 radical feminist lesbians.

1972

The first UK Pride march takes place in London on 1st July, the nearest Saturday to the anniversary of the Stonewall Riots.

1974

The London Lesbian and Gay Switchboard opens, offering confidential advice and information for queer people, by queer people, for free.

1978

Harvey Milk, one of the first openly gay elected officials in the US, is assassinated.

1979

Liverpool holds its first Gay Pride Week.

1984

Labour MP Chris Smith becomes the first British politician to come out as gay. In 1997, he becomes the first out cabinet minister.

2005

The Gender Recognition Act comes into force in the UK, allowing trans people to legally change their gender and acquire new birth certificates.

2010

The It Gets Better movement is created in the US to give messages of hope to LGBTQ+ youth through storytelling and education.

2013

Bayard Rustin is posthumously awarded the Presidential Medal of Freedom. He was a gay Black man and Martin Luther King Jr.'s right-hand man, who brought the AIDS crisis to Black leaders' attention.

2023

Protests take place at Tate Britain art gallery during Drag Queen Story Hour.

2023

Vigils are held for murdered trans teen Brianna Ghey.

2023

Nearly 1,000 contributors at the *New York Times* sign an open letter condemning the paper for anti-trans reporting.

Age of Consent Around the World

The legal age of consent for same-sex partners is often an indicator of how progressive a country is.

Laws around same-sex activity come down to two points:

1. Are LGBTQ+ people allowed to have sex at all?
2. If sex is allowed, from what age can it happen (the age of consent)?

All legal sex requires consent – regardless of who it happens between, everyone involved must agree to it freely. The age of consent is the age a person can legally take part in sexual activity. These laws are designed to protect young people around the world. For years in the UK, a big deal was rightly made over the LGBTQ+ 'age of consent' because the laws were so discriminatory. Until 1994, if you wanted to have LGBTQ+ sex, you had to wait till you were 21, even though the age of consent for heterosexual couples was 16 (see page 41). Fortunately, most countries that allow LGBTQ+ activity now have an equal age of consent – but what that age is still varies.

Sadly, some countries forbid gay sex altogether and have banned any same-sex activity. Some countries have even criminalised just discussing LGBTQ+ rights (see page 40).

Quick stats

- 171 countries have an equal age of consent for gay and straight sex
- 39 countries do not have equal age of consent laws for gay and straight sex
- At least 65 countries criminalise same-sex sexual activity
- At least 38 countries criminalise sex between women
- 14 countries criminalise non-normative gender expression

The following countries are just a few of those where the age of consent is the same for same-sex and straight partners. The average global age of consent is 16.

Laws are changing all the time. In 2022 alone, six countries or regions equalised the age of consent. However, there remain inequalities. Madagascar currently has one of the starkest: the general age of consent is 14, rising to 21 for same-sex relationships.

Criminalising queerness

You never know where you will come across homophobia, but in some countries, it's written into law. All of the following ban same-sex relationships: **Malaysia, Bangladesh, Syria, Egypt, Pakistan, Iraq, Algeria, Qatar, Kuwait, Morocco, Zimbabwe, Oman, Kenya, Ethiopia, Tanzania, Papua New Guinea, Guyana, Myanmar, Liberia, Somalia.** They aren't the only ones – there are currently at least 65 countries that criminalise same-sex relationships.

And it gets worse. Well into the 21st century, there are some nations where being queer is punishable by death:

Iran – In 2019, a man was hanged for breaking anti-gay laws.
Nigeria – LGBTQ+ people can face prison or death by stoning.
Saudi Arabia – Those caught more than once can face the death penalty.
Afghanistan – Sharia Law means that gay men and women can be killed to 'restore the honour of the family'.
Sudan – Has a 'three strikes and then we kill you' law.
United Arab Emirates – You can be hanged, but jail sentences or fines are more common punishments.

Try looking online for LGBTQ+ travel resources if you need advice – and be aware of the laws and cultural attitudes in the countries you visit. Remember: some countries may have really strict anti-LGBTQ+ laws, but it doesn't mean all the people there will be homophobic.

Spotlight on the UK

The road to sexual equality in the UK has been bumpy. But we got there eventually . . .

1275 – The age of consent for heterosexual sex is set for the first time at 12 years old.

1875 – The age of consent is raised to 13.

1885 – The age of consent is raised to 16 in a bid to protect children from prostitution.

1917 – A bill is proposed to raise the age to 17, but it is defeated.

1967 – The first age of consent for gay men is set at 21. Before this, it was illegal for gay men to have sex at all.

1994 – The age of consent for gay men is lowered to 18.

2000 – The age is lowered again, to 16 – bringing it in line with straight sex age of consent. Finally.

ASSUMPTION SMASH

Laws against lesbians and gay men in the UK have always been the same

No – there has never been legislation against two women having sex in the UK. Rumour has it that when it was proposed in the 1800s, Queen Victoria refused to believe lesbians existed. I doubt that's true. She was probably dismissive because thinking about other people's sex lives was a weird preoccupation at the time and she didn't want to get involved.

Allyship

Queer history isn't just for queer people, it's for everyone. Lesser-known facts about LGBTQ+ culture round out our knowledge, and that's interesting for ALL of us. If you're straight and you care about gay rights (if that's NOT you, I'm amazed you've made it this far), here are ten top ways to be a good ally.

1. Use the right words. Expanding your LGBTQ+ vocab is a great start, go back to page 15 for a refresher. Remember that terms are changing all the time.
2. Use the right pronouns. If you don't know, ask!
3. Try not to assume straightness. People often ask girls if they have a crush on a boy. But if we're going to get personal, we should keep language neutral. "Got any crushes?" Allow a space for non-conforming expression.
4. Read widely. There are tonnes of LGBTQ+ books out there – oh, look, you're holding one already! There are whole bookshops devoted to queer writing, like the amazing intersectional queer bookshop/café/community hub Common Press in London.
5. Support queer-run businesses. Have a shop around next time you run out of moisturiser/tea towels/chocolate buttons and find an LGBTQ+ supplier.
6. Accept that you might say the wrong thing. True, celebrities can get cancelled for it, but in a private setting, it's rarely the end of the world. Wanting to do the right thing, and apologising where needed, counts for a lot.
7. If you notice a friend laughing at a homophobic joke, call

them out. That said, make sure you feel safe to do so, and remember that shaming people in public (including on the internet and social media) often does more harm than good. Oh and don't use 'gay' as a word to describe something cringe, lame or rubbish.

8. Don't expect people to conform to the societal norms that *you're* comfortable with – others might not be.
9. Be inclusive. Investigate some corners of the community you don't know as much about.
10. Amplify LGBTQ+ voices wherever you can (without speaking *for* queer people).

Straight stars we stan

In the queer community, there's an ongoing discourse about the fact that straight women make up the vast majority of the celebrities we obsess over, musicians who we listen to, and actors we can't get enough of. Sometimes, it seems that we prefer these straight women over actual LGBTQ+ artists. While this might partly be true, you could argue that the majority of people are straight, so there's more of them to stan, and queer people have never been afforded the same visibility. Historically, women have stood as avatars for a lot of gay men, allowing us to vicariously live through them – from Cher to Katherine Hepburn to Cate Blanchett. They have strong but playful personas that let us know that they're not only cool with us, but will defend us to the death. As homophobia dies, more and more entertainers come out, we will naturally stan more queer stars. It's already happening with *Drag Race* alum such as Trixie and Katya, actors including Jonathan Bailey and Kristen Stewart, and comedy treasures such as Kate McKinnon and Bowen Yang.

Dates for Your Diary

JANUARY

- Veganuary
- 16th–20th – No Name-Calling Week
- 27th – Holocaust Remembrance Day

FEBRUARY

- LGBTQ+ History Month
- Aromantic Spectrum Awareness Week
- Sydney Mardi Gras (starts on the second Thursday of the month)

MAY

- 7th – International Day Against Homophobia, Transphobia and Biphobia
- 19th – Agender Pride Day
- 22nd – Harvey Milk Day
- Eurovision month
- 28th – Kylie's birthday

JUNE

- Pride Month
- 12th – Pulse Night of Remembrance
- 28th – Beginning of Stonewall Riots anniversary period
- Gay Days at Disney (first Saturday in June)

SEPTEMBER

- 4th – Beyoncé's birthday
- 16th–22nd – Bisexual Awareness Week
- 23rd – Celebrate Bisexuality Day

OCTOBER

- Black History Month
- 8th – International Lesbian Day
- 11th – National Coming Out Day
- 17th – International Pronouns Day
- 26th – Intersex Awareness Day

Homophobia is real, but there's PLENTY in the LGBTQ+ calendar to counteract it. Why not create a bespoke version with dates that are important to YOU.

MARCH	APRIL
• 1st – Zero Discrimination Day • 28th – Lady Gaga's birthday • 31st – International Transgender Day of Visibility	• 6th – International Asexuality Day • 26th – Lesbian Visibility Day • 30th – Anniversary of the Admiral Duncan pub bombing in 1999

JULY	AUGUST
• Pride in London (first Saturday of the month) • UK Black Pride • Crop top season • 14th – International Non-Binary People's Day	• Manchester Pride • Gay Uncle Day (second Sunday of the month) • 16th – Madonna's birthday

NOVEMBER	DECEMBER
• Trans Awareness Month • 8th – Intersex Day of Remembrance • 20th – Transgender Day of Remembrance • 23rd – Polyamory Day	• 1st – World AIDS Day • 8th – Pansexual Pride Day • 10th – Human Rights Day • Mariah season

Cracking the Queer Code

In times when same-sex desire was criminalised, symbols became important ways of signalling that you were . . . y'know. Some of these symbols have been adopted over the years as ways for people to joyfully broadcast their identity, whether loudly and proudly, or in a more subtle way.

Rainbow

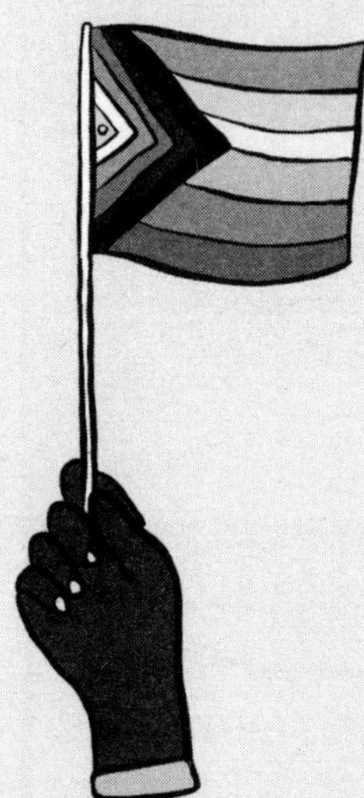

Adopted by: The LGBTQ+ community

When?: 1970s

It wasn't until 1978 that the rainbow flag, designed by Gilbert Baker, came to be adopted as the universal symbol for queer pride. The rainbow flag was originally designed to have eight colours, each representing a wonderful, if somewhat hippyish, aspect of life. Pink represented sex, red was for life, orange healing, yellow the Sun, green nature, turquoise for art and magic, blue serenity and purple represented the spirit. Pretty groovy, baby.

In 2018, non-binary American artist Daniel Quasar designed the Progress Pride Flag, to specifically include people of colour and the trans and non-binary community. The creator assigned a double meaning to the black stripe, which recognises both the Black queer community and those who have died from, and are living with, AIDS.

Adopted by: The trans community

When?: 1990s

The Venus and Mars symbols work so well that they just needed to be tweaked to represent people with a trans experience. The new version, conceived by Holly Boswell, combines male and female symbols and also adds an extra part that combines both.

Adopted by: Lesbians and gay men

When?: 1970s

The 11th letter of the Greek alphabet was used to represent gay liberation in the early 70s, but the reason behind the choice isn't that clear. Good job the rainbow flag came along.

Adopted by: Lesbians

When?: 1970s

Lesbian women in the 70s wanted a strong and powerful symbol to represent them. The mythical double-headed axe of the Greek goddess Artemis and her Amazon warriors was perfect.

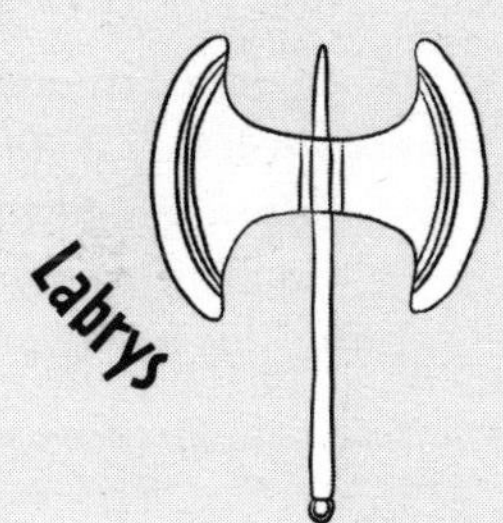

Hanky code

Adopted by: Gay men and lesbians

When?: 1970s and 80s

A cute bandana in your back pocket used to be more than an accessory – it was a way to let people know what you were 'into' years before online dating profiles. Different colours meant different things, let's just say that.

Violet

Adopted by: Lesbians

When?: Since about the 1920s

Ancient Greek mother of lesbians, Sappho, wrote of decorating hair with violets. In contemporary times, the trend started with the opening of a play by Édouard Bourdet – a lesbian character sends a bouquet of these small purple flowers to her lover. Viola is also a cross-dressing heroine in Shakespeare's most sexually fluid play, *Twelfth Night* (see page 167).

Green carnation

Adopted by: Gay men

When?: Late 1800s

Green carnations were beautiful but totally unnatural: they were specially dyed green rather than growing that way. Oscar Wilde made them 'a thing' and you had to get them from one particular florist in London, called Goodyear's.

Peacock feather

Adopted by: Gay men

When?: 1800s

The look-at-me fabulousness of the peacock is almost too obvious, but gay men in the 19th century said, "No such thing, dear."

Queer Spaces

Queer Spaces: Why So Important?

Throughout history, like-minded queers have come together to escape the repressive stressors of mainstream culture, form secret societies, and become friends, lovers, rivals and role models.

'Queer spaces' are important in ways we don't always think about. Because the world is often a complete buzzkill for us, we have to find somewhere we can be ourselves, without fear of tuts. These spaces can be buildings, businesses, clubs – even entire neighbourhoods. In the 1920s, Harlem, New York City and Bloomsbury, London, were queer hubs. Today, LGBTQ+ travellers might choose Le Marais in Paris, or Fire Island in New York. And queer spaces are always shifting and changing – every generation is looking for their own unique place to express themselves. It could be a sports club, TikTok, a café – anywhere you feel safe and included. My places used to be nightclubs like Smashing and Popstarz, Duckie and Boombox. These days, my personal queer spaces are often The Common Press and Gay's The Word bookshops, The National Gallery, Highgate men's pond and just about every Hackney coffee shop.

Over the next chapter, we'll traipse through some of the most iconic hidden places, where queer people past and present have been free to live their best lives, feel valued and inspired, explore themselves, and – almost certainly – each other.

Queer-only spaces?

Places that shut out certain types of people have a pretty tricksy job of convincing us why. Sure, I've been to queer nights that have become victims of their own success and slowly morphed into straight nights. So annoying. But I don't believe in not letting straight people into queer-run clubs if they're going with queer friends. How do you prove queerness anyway? The problem starts if you dictate that only certain types of person are acceptable. Then it's like being bullied all over again and it's bye-bye safe space, hiya hierarchy.

I remember once going out to Le Queen, the biggest gay club in Paris – and not getting in because I wasn't gay enough. This isn't a bro-ish humble brag. I was too unkempt for the pristine Parisian gatekeepers. I kissed my boyfriend to prove my allegiance, but they didn't buy it. The next night we went back, and this time I wore tight white jeans and a tiny T-shirt. We swished straight in, *naturellement*. Today, that compromise seems weak-willed and I'm almost ashamed – but it illustrates that even queer spaces can be exclusionary.

Popular places to find queer people

Department stores, Carly Rae Jepsen concerts, art shows, vegan cafés, hotel bars, libraries, Wimbledon tennis matches, Eurovision, churches, the army, premier league football games, National Trust tea rooms, art supply stores, indoor climbing walls, graveyards . . . You get the picture. Baby, we're everywhere.

A-Z of Queer Spaces

"Find your tribe," they say.
"Where?" you say. "Here!" we say.

Angela Burdett-Coutts Memorial Fountain and Sundial, St Pancras Old Church, London

A lesbian-built memorial to people who were buried here but removed – including the gender-non-conforming hero/heroine the Chevalier d'Eon (see page 90).

Bishopsgate Institute, LGBTQ+ Archives, London

Book an appointment to see their whopping great collection of queer artifacts and ephemera.

Castro district, San Francisco

There are gay villages, and then there's The Castro, the daddy of queer spaces, and the US's first (and best?) gaybourhood.

Dungeness, Kent

A town on the heel of Kent, where patron saint of the avant-garde Derek Jarman made his home, Prospect Cottage, right next to a nuclear power plant. So emo. He lived there until he died from AIDS complications in 1994.

Elia Beach, Mykonos

The lesbians have their Grecian paradise, Lesbos, and the gays have Mykonos. In high season they flock to clothing-optional Elia beach. #BlushesInGreek

Frida Kahlo Museum, Mexico City

One of the best house and garden museums in the world, packed with Kahlo's personal possessions and art.

Georgen Parochial Protestant Cemetery, Berlin

This German burial ground has its own 40-square-metre lesbian section.

Hebden Bridge, West Yorkshire

The beautiful mill town is a queer haven some call 'the lesbian capital of the UK'.

Iceland

Iceland is not even slightly frosty when it comes to the LGBTQ+ community. In 2015 the homeland of our lady Björk was ranked the no. 1 happiest place to live by gay men.

Jersey Heritage Museum, Jersey

View works by surrealist artist, gender-non-conforming, anti-Nazi resistance fighter Claude Cahun.

Knole, Kent

The National Trust childhood home of renowned posho queero Vita Sackville-West. The sprawling estate inspired Virginia Woolf's 'trans' novel *Orlando*.

Lighthouse Bookshop, Edinburgh

A queer-owned, women-led community bookstore.

Montevergine, Campania, Italy

Every year on 2nd February, queer, trans and third-gender Italians make the pilgrimage to visit the 'Black Madonna', a 13th-century 'LGBTQ+ saint'.

Neuschwanstein Castle, Bavaria, Germany

Ludwig II was gay as a goose and rich beyond imagining. His fairytale castle was the inspiration for the castle in Disney's *Sleeping Beauty*.

Oscar Wilde memorial statue, London

Lesbian artist Maggi Hambling's unmissable sculpture encourages passers-by to sit with the greatest wit that was.

Plas Newydd, Llangollen, Wales

The 18th-century home of the scandalous 'Ladies of Llangollen', a pair of women who lived together for 50 years, wore men's hats and named ALL their dogs 'Sappho'.

Queer Britain Museum, Granary Square, London

Britain's first LGBTQ+ museum opened in 2022.

Rosa Bonheur, Buttes-Chaumont, Paris

The only nightclub on this list – because it's so much more than that. It's an early Sunday evening queer social club in a Paris park, named after the animal-painter genius.

Shibden Hall, Halifax

Anne Lister's country pile. An essential stop for *Gentleman Jack* enthusiasts.

Taormina, Sicily

A popular queer holiday spot at the turn of the 20th century, the town still attracts well-heeled homos.

Una Troubridge's house, Rye

Sculptor Una and her author partner, Radclyffe Hall, lived together in the sleepy East Sussex town of Rye, home to several other lesbian/trans masc residents.

Villa Lysis, Capri, Italy

A beautiful villa built in 1904 by Count Fersen, who lived with his model boyfriend Nino Cesarini. If the sunken baths (yes, there's more than one) could talk!

Wakefield Street, London

Pay homage to infamous music-hall cross-dressers Stella and Fanny at their commemorative blue plaque.

Xilitla, Las Pozas, Mexico

In the heart of the Mexican jungle lies a fantastical sculpture garden created by gay surrealist Edward James.

Yumbo Centre, Gran Canaria

The official website calls it 'the one and only LGBTI shopping centre in the world'. That's not even the half of it.

Zona Romántica, Puerto Vallarta, Mexico

Mexico's LGBTQ+-friendly resort is so popular that its fans just call it PV.

Join the Club

Focusing on an activity, whether online or in person, helps break the ice in social situations – you don't have to talk unless you want to. The clubs here give a taste of the UK's diverse queer hangouts.

Roller derby

Try Auld Reekie Women's Roller Derby in Edinburgh – for anyone identifying as female.

Books

Google 'LGBTQ+ book club'. There are tons of intersectional ones, like Queer Reads Book Club in Bristol.

Yoga

Lunges in Leggings, in London is one of the funnest ways to work up a sweat. Lycra not compulsory.

Gaming

London Gaymers is a gaming social club where members hold online tournaments and meet up monthly. For LGBTQ+ women or non-binaries, try Sappho Events.

Swimming

If you're trans or non-binary, try Trans Active in Sheffield.

Gardening

Look out for events held by Queer Botany.

Martial arts

Try Ishikagi Ju-Jitsu, the UK's largest LGBTQ+ martial arts club.

Badminton, squash and tennis

Ace your serve at Rainbow Raquets in Leicester.

Online networks

OK, it's not a club as such – but there's a sub-Reddit for everything. If you ever feel alone or confused, you can bet that someone on the LGBTeens thread has been there, done that, and posted all about it.

Outdoor activities

Like getting into the countryside? Try Active Out Exeter.

Dancing

Kick up the sawdust with Manchester Prairie Dogs Line Dancing. Yee-haw!

Football

Try the Gay Football Supporters Network League. They have teams in cities across the UK, including Belfast Blaze FC, the only LGBTQ+ football team in Northern Ireland.

Vogueing

Open to 15–25 year olds, Nottingham Contemporary holds classes in Ballroom.

Places to Be Gay Famous

Queer people own the night; we always have. When you're not welcome in the mainstream world, it's not a bad idea to create your own when everyone else is in bed. At night, we're free to be ourselves, away from basic prying eyes.

Andy Warhol kickstarted the idea of a star system outside mainstream celebrity, making 'superstars' of his 'discoveries'. Today, most major cities have their own stars of the night: the people who waltz into any place they fancy and get treated like royalty. If you could join a gang of infamous queer night owls, who'd you pick? Choose a time, a place and a cute look, and enter your Club Kid era . . .

1960s and 70s

The Cockettes

Where: The Palace Theatre, San Francisco.

Who: Hibiscus, Sweet Pam, Scrumbly, Sylvester, Fayette

Do: A radical performance piece inspired by silent movies . . . in just your pants.

Wear: Glitter in your beard, caked-on make-up, bangles.

Legacy: Gender F-word drag.

1970s

Antonio Lopez's glam gang

Where: Club Sept in Paris.

Who: Pat Cleveland, Grace Jones, Juan Ramos, Tina Chow, Donna Jordan, Jane Forth, Corey Grant Tippin.

Do: Sketch beautiful fashion illustrations of your model friends then jet to Saint-Tropez.

Wear: Couture, prêt-a-porter, Chanel, Yves Saint Laurent.

Legacy: Bisexual fashion illustrator Antonio Lopez showed that fantasy beats reality.

1980s

Leigh Bowery's art-pop drag freaks

Where: Taboo nightclub, Leicester Square, London.

Who: Boy George, Trojan, Sue Tilley, Princess Julia, Lanah Pellay, Michael Clark, Phillip Salon, Nicola Bowery, Matthew Glamorre, Marilyn.

Do: Have fun and scare the bejeez out of the neighbours

Wear: Egg-splat head, blue body paint, lumpy tights.

Legacy: Leigh Bowery's 'living art' inspired everyone from Lady Gaga to Alexander McQueen.

1980s and 90s

NYC Club Kids

Where: Disco 2000 at Limelight, New York.

Who: RuPaul, Lady Bunny, James St. James, Amanda Lepore, Susanne Bartsch, Larry Tee, Michael Alig, Clara the Carefree Chicken, Chloë Sevigny, Zaldy, Jenny Talia, Nelson Sullivan.

Do: Stay up all night showing off your looks.

Wear: Ugly glamour, onesies, romper-suits, animal costumes, troll hair, fake noses and everything you robbed from Leigh Bowery.

Legacy: The Club Kids took their chaotic aesthetic to the limit and it paid off big time for RuPaul.

2000s

The T-Shack girlies

Where: The Stud in San Francisco.

Who: From drag queens and trans icons like founder Heklina and Holly Woodlawn to pop royalty Lady Gaga and Gwen Stefani to regular host Ana Matronic.

Do: Rip up the rule book and test the boundaries of gender and bad taste.

Wear: DIY drag.

Legacy: Before the T-slur word was erased from our collective language, before drag was everywhere, T-Shack gave queers and allies a safe space to perform and go wild.

2010s

Sink The Pinkers

Where: From the original Sink The Pink club in East London to New York, Brazil and beyond.

Who: Founders Amy Zing and Glyn Fussell, plus Jacqui Potato, Jade Thirlwall, Jodie Harsh and Olly Alexander and also Asttina Mandela and Bimini Bon Boulash who won both won Miss Sink The Pink years before they entered *Drag Race UK*.

Do: Run around like a kid who ate all the Haribo and dance to Whigfield.

Wear: Something frilly and glittery that cost you 50p.

Legacy: Sink The Pink did the thing, and in 2017 created the UK's best queer music festival, Mighty Hoopla, and it's so good and so popular that it's weird no one ever did it before. In 2022, Glyn published *Manifesto For Misfits*. Go dance, go read! Go!

2020s

House of Avalon

Where: In an apartment somewhere in East Hollywood.

Who: Gigi Goode, Symone, Marko Monroe, Hunter Crenshaw, Rylie, Grant Vanderbilt, Caleb Feeney, Rubberchild.

Do: Worship in the church of pop culture by day. Create playgrounds from the imagination by night.

Wear: A gorgeous couture piece made by Jeremy Scott, or better yet, Gigi's mum.

Legacy: Avalon TV launched on WowPresentsPlus in October 2023.

Roaring Cities: London, Berlin, Paris

Over the years, some cities have gained a reputation as havens for queers. Hop on a plane and jump in a time machine . . . let's visit three cities where it's great to be queer, now and centuries ago.

LONDON

The Bloomsbury Group

If you're looking for the most complicated love lives of any group ever, look no further than the Bloomsbury Group. This set of intellectuals were sort of related, mostly bisexual, and couldn't keep their hands off each other. The art they created was just as free and expressive. They lived around Bloomsbury in London – cos, duh!

Who: The painter Duncan Grant and his cousin Lytton Strachey, Vanessa Bell and her author sister Virginia Woolf, the economist John Maynard Keynes, artist Dora Carrington, writer E. M. Forster.

Watch: *Orlando* (PG) with Tilda Swinton and the BBC show *Life in Squares* (15) with James Norton as Duncan Grant.

Read: *Mrs Dalloway* by Virginia Woolf, *Maurice* by E. M. Forster and *Deceived With Kindness* by Angelica Garnett.

Bright Young Things

The less-serious London upper-crusties who found the Bloomsbury Group a bit stuffy. These guys were the celebutantes of the day, pursued by the press from season to season, party to party. Favourite hangouts were the Cavendish Hotel and the Gargoyle members club in Soho, designed by Matisse and Lutyens.

Who: Photographer Cecil Beaton, writer Nancy Mitford and her sister Diana, playwright Noel Coward, poet John Betjeman, Stephen Tennant, Lady Caroline Paget and Howard Acton.

Watch: The movie *Bright Young Things* (15), directed by Stephen Fry, and the BBC's *Pursuit of Love* (12) with Lily James and Andrew Scott.

Read: *Vile Bodies* by Evelyn Waugh and *Love in a Cold Climate* by Nancy Mitford.

London today

London still holds its own when it comes to queer living. Soho used to be the only place to go, but now the East End is almost more fun – the area around Broadway Market in Hackney is starting to feel like an LGBTQ+ village. The city attracts queer people from all over the world, making it an incredibly exciting place to be. London is arguably the gayest city in Europe, with inclusive events for every identity.

BERLIN

Life Is a Cabaret

From 1918 to 1933 – between the two world wars and before the Nazis destroyed the city's queer culture – Berlin was a decadent city where gay nightlife thrived. In the mid 1920s, there were over 50 lesbian bars! Like New York City, Berlin was famous for its extravagant queer balls, where gentlemen were known to wear full drag with elegant moustaches, and the ladies were suited and bow-tied up to their sharply cut bobs.

Who: German cabaret stars like Marlene Dietrich and Claire Waldoff blurred gender boundaries, while queer English writers W. H. Auden, Stephen Spender and Christopher Isherwood scribbled down everything they saw. Weimarvellous, darlink.

Watch: The films *The Blue Angel* (U), *I Am a Camera* (12) and *Cabaret* (15).

Read: *Goodbye to Berlin* by Christopher Isherwood, *The Temple* by Stephen Spender.

Berlin today

Today, Berlin is one of the top destinations for queer travellers, especially those wanting to explore avant-garde contemporary art and the legendary club scene. It's super-relaxed when it comes to queer identities and has some of the best parties. #TechnoTechnoTechno

PARIS
Left Bank Lesbians

We think of Berlin as being the most decadent city, but don't sleep on Paris, once known as 'Paris Lesbos' thanks to – well, you can guess. First, there were the legendary salons (civilised parties) of Gertrude Stein and her partner Alice B. Toklas, frequented by Picasso and F. Scott Fitzgerald. Queer clubs, cafés and bars were also *de rigueur*. At Le Monocle, the chicest spot for gay *filles*, you might run into Fat Claude, one of the first trans men to have gender-affirming surgery.

Who: Gertrude Stein, Alice B. Toklas, Dolly Wilde, Colette, Josephine Baker, Jean Cocteau and André Gide. Not to forget Barbette, the incandescent drag queen of the Moulin Rouge.

Watch: The movies *Midnight in Paris* (13) and *Victor/ Victoria* (15) with Julie Andrews, said to have been inspired by the success of Barbette.

Read: *Three Lives* by Gertrude Stein, *Les Enfants Terribles* by Jean Cocteau, *Chéri* by Colette.

Paris today

There's so much romance in Paris that everyone should go and explore. The famous (bourgeois?) gay hub Le Marais is perhaps past its prime, so branch out and explore cooler, lesser-known neighbourhoods like Belleville in the 19th and 20th *arrondissements*.

Black Queer Spaces: Harlem Renaissance

In the 1920s and 30s, uptown New York fizzed with a flourishing Black queer community.

When WWI was out of the way, modern life as we know it could begin. The scene was set for the Harlem Renaissance, an explosion of Black culture in North Manhattan, New York, from 1919 to 1937. 'The Great Migration' from the entrenched racism of the rural south to northern cities of the US brought with it writers, musicians, painters and performers eager to express their experience as African-Americans, forge a new Black identity, advocate for civil rights and, in some cases, sexual liberation. Their downtown white neighbours were fascinated by the hot new subcultures being created – blues, jazz, theatre, dance, spoken-word poetry – and they flocked to Harlem to be a part of them. However, the most popular 'straight' venues like the Cotton Club promoted Black performers while banning Black patrons, so queer POCs had to find other places to be free.

Hamilton Lodge (W. 155th Street and 8th Avenue)

The famous Hamilton Lodge 'fairy balls' were once-a-year, traffic-stopping events that could be considered some of the first queer club nights. In 1929, Black journalist Gerri Major nailed the attraction of the balls:

"The greatest joy in life is to be able to express one's inner self. The second greatest joy is to be able to mingle with one's kind."

The Dark Tower (108 W. 136th Street)

A'Lelia Walker, aka The Mahogany Millionairess aka 'The Joy Goddess of Harlem', held salons called 'The Dark Tower'. The heiress to a Black haircare business, she would serve caviar and champagne to artists and writers, including Langston Hughes, Zora Neale Hurston and Carl Van Vechten – at a time when booze was prohibited. Hughes wrote that A'Lelia's parties "were as crowded as the New York subway at rush hour".

Gumby Book Studio (2144 Fifth Avenue)

Alexander Gumby, or 'The Great God Gumby', opened queer literary salon Gumby Book Studio in 1926. A collector and archivist of African-American history, he hosted parties, performances and exhibitions dedicated to the leading lights of the Harlem Renaissance.

Harry Hansberry's Clam House (133rd Street)

A gay and lesbian speakeasy where the booming voice of Gladys Bentley in white top hat and tails reigned supreme. Gladys would sing her unique and bawdy songs from ten till dawn backed by dancers in drag. Celebrities and socialites flocked to witness her drag king persona.

Harlem Renaissance Cast List

Langston Hughes

The gay poet laureate of Harlem.

Ma Rainey

Queen of the Blues, a brilliant singer and proud out lesbian.

Bessie Smith

Bessie toured with Ma Rainey and was a sensational singer in her own right, gaining the nickname 'Empress of the Blues'.

Wallace Thurman

Novelist famous for his exploration of colourism (discrimination against people of different skin tones).

Gladys Bentley

Lesbian singer who performed in white tux and top hat butch-drag.

Countee Cullen

The most famous Black writer of the 1920s.

Jimmie Daniels

Gay cabaret singer and nightclub owner.

Zora Neale Hurston

Celebrated writer and central figure of the Harlem Renaissance.

Ethel Waters

Actress, singer, and only the second Black person to be nominated for an Oscar.

Harold Jackman

A school teacher dubbed 'The handsomest man in Harlem'.

Richard Bruce Nugent

Out writer, artist and 'gay rebel of the Harlem Renaissance'.

Edna Thomas

One of the first Black actresses on the New York stage.

Richmond Barthé

The first African-American sculptor to receive major acclaim.

Carl Van Vechten

White promoter and photographer of the Harlem Renaissance.

Black Queer Spaces: The Ballroom

As a wide-eyed teen in the pre-internet 90s, learning about queer culture was a sketchy affair. So when my friends and I found a VHS tape of *Paris Is Burning*, the 1980s documentary about Ballroom, we watched it until the tape wore out.

RuPaul's *Drag Race* references Ballroom culture nearly every episode with its use of slang and vogueing dance moves – but Ballroom is so much more than dips and duck-walks. Ballroom was a dance contest, a beauty pageant and a world where queer Black and Latinx people found refuge – the original safe space. *Paris Is Burning* transforms the most marginalised people in society into something eternally glamorous and iconic. It has given us a fun queer lexicon with words like shade, reading, work, gag and Kiki while teaching us serious lessons about race, gender, class, capitalism, community, family, fragile masculinity, sexuality and survival. Survival of the sickest.

Crystal kicks it off

The birth of Ballroom can be traced back to the very first queer masquerade ball held at Hamilton Lodge in Harlem, New York City, in 1869. The scene exploded during the Harlem Renaissance of the 1920s and 30s, when drag balls held once a year featured a 'parade of the fairies', competing for the best look.

As the scene progressed, Houses started to appear – family-like groups run by 'mothers' and 'fathers'. Crystal LaBeija is said to have originated the House system in the mid 1970s, throwing the first ball, as we think of them today, with fellow Harlem drag artist Lottie.

In another seminal queer documentary, *The Queen* (1968), LaBeija gives us an insight into why balls and the House system had to come into being. She vents her frustration after a simpering white girl called Harlow wins a pageant over more-deserving Black girls. If the perception was 'beauty pageants are rigged', you can understand the need to build a system that gives all competitors a fighting chance. And the House system did just that.

To be real, to be now

Films like *Paris Is Burning* and *The Queen* freeze moments in time, but the Ballroom scene gallops on apace and now major cities all over the world have thriving Ballroom and Kiki (smaller party) scenes. Jay Jay Revlon, a leading figure in London's ball scene told me recently:

"*Paris Is Burning* is educational, in terms of history and categories, but in terms of the scene, it's not a very clear representation of what's going on now."

If you want an idea of where Ballroom is today, including must-see performances, try looking on TikTok (where else?). There are vogue nights and balls happening everywhere from Paris to Berlin, Toronto to Tokyo, and even dance classes you can take. Remember, though, that Ballroom was born out of marginalised queer people of colour's need for a safe, accepting space. If you ever decide to go to a ball (and I recommend it if you can), look for one that values this, and be aware of your own position there. If everyone in the room is white or straight or cis, then the dynamic is irrevocably altered, potentially alienating the people that Ballroom celebrates. When trans actress Dominique Jackson was starring in the TV show *Pose*, she made it absolutely clear why the Ballroom community was her refuge and escape from a harsh world:

"The Ballroom had to happen because we needed to find a place, because we had no place to belong and no place to go and find camaraderie and community and enjoy ourselves [. . .] once you're in that ballroom space you're so happy, you're so free, you're with your friends, your peers, mothers, fathers – it's magic to me."

From her words, you can see that Ballroom wasn't just a cute party, or a nightclub to hang out in and dance and compete, it was a community-focused space. A place that had to be created, because it didn't exist in the mainstream world. As a trans woman of colour, Dominique not only faced discrimination on the daily, but also the very real threat of violence. For her and others, ballroom was – and still is – the ultimate queer safe space.

Michelle Visage gave good face

Drag Race judge Michelle Visage is said to be the first cis woman to walk at a ball. She was taught to vogue by OG vogue father, Willi Ninja. Vogueing featured in the video to Michelle's hit single *Two to Make It Right* with girl group Seduction. The song was released in November 1989, just months before Madonna's *Vogue*, which came out March the next year.

House of Ninja

Willi Ninja has been described as the godfather of vogueing. He grew up in New York in the 60s and 70s, falling in love with ballet, Fred Astaire and kung fu films – which is how he got his name. Born William Roscoe Leake, Willi started hanging out on the Christopher Street pier, before taking his skills indoors to the balls, forming the House of Ninja in 1982. The creation of vogueing is often credited to drag artist Paris Dupree, but Willi Ninja took it to the masses. Willi Ninja's signature moves, characterised by elegant arm-control, contortion, locking, balance and mime, are still to be found in Ballroom today.

Ballroom for beginners

Runway contestant categories

Femme queen (FQ) – trans women
Butch queen (BQ) – gay or bi cis men
Butch – masculine-presenting women
Male figure (MF) – anyone presenting as male
Female figure (FF) – anyone presenting as female
Open to all (OTA) – anyone can walk

Spot the legendary Houses

Aviance, Balenciaga, Balmain, Corey, Ebony, Escada, Evisu, Garcon, Gucci, Icon, Khan, LaBeija, Milan, Miyake-Mugler, Mizrahi, Ninja, Pendavis, Revlon, St Laurent, Tisci, West, Xtravaganza.

Categories you might see at a ball

Vogue femme
Old way/new way
Hand performance
European runway
All-American runway
Face
Body
Sex siren
Realness
Realness with a twist
Bizarre

WTF History

Labelling the Past

Why do we presume that historical figures are straight?

When film director Francis Lee was promoting his film *Ammonite,* with Kate Winslet and Saoirse Ronan playing lesbian fossil hunters, people got mad. Winslet's character, Mary Anning, was a real person and she couldn't have been a lesbian – could she? Maybe she had female friends, we all do, but does that make us ALL lesbians?!? Under the right circumstances, probably. When looking at Anning's life in early-1800s England, Francis Lee unsurprisingly didn't find much about her sexuality, so built out a story. But why should Winslet's character HAVE to be straight? Why is straight the automatic default?

The concept of identifying as bi, lesbian, trans – or anything other than straight – did not exist until about 120 years ago. That's not to say that a queer sensibility didn't exist though – we know it did. Same-sex love has been around since we were plankton (I fact-checked this), but societal pressures meant that unless you were a king, you would've had to *pretend* to be straight. Because of this lack of openness in history, we will never know for sure what goes on in the hearts and beds of dead people – we can only speculate.

Denial of all possible queerness in our historical figures isn't just homophobic, it's nonsensical. If it was once illegal to eat apples and the world was filled with apple trees, you might assume that apples would still be consumed regularly, if somewhat secretly. Historians tell us that apples remained on the trees, no one ever wanted one, that it was a sin to pick them and people preferred oranges anyway. But we know very well that oranges aren't the only fruit.

Do tell . . .

Queerness is often invisible. We need to talk about it in order to know it exists. Not discussing queerness is an active denial and suppression. If you stand in front of a Frida Kahlo painting, you can see she's a woman of colour, you might spot her disability, but unless they tell us she had relationships with women, we will never know. I've spent hours in exhibitions and watching films where the person's life and work is explored without ever mentioning the fact that they were like me. The curators and creators denied me an opportunity to connect with the work on a personal level and see patterns that relate to my own experiences. We can do better!

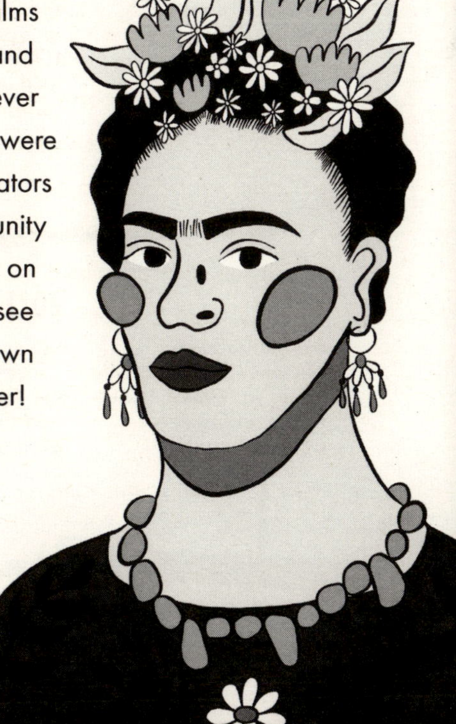

first!

At first we were afraid, we were petrified . . . But then, slowly . . . progress. Here are some fascinating LGBTQ+ firsts from the last century.

1978

In Australia, the first Sydney Gay and Lesbian Mardi Gras takes place.

1978

The rainbow flag flies for the first time – at the San Francisco Gay Freedom Day parade.

1973

Jobriath, the first openly gay rock star, releases his self-titled first album. Put 'I'm a Man' on your gym playlist now.

1982

Terrence Higgins is the first British gay man to be diagnosed with, and die of, an AIDS-related illness.

1982

The First Gay Games, an event held for LGBTQ+ athletes, is held in San Francisco (where else?).

1988

The first World AIDS Day is observed on 1st December.

2022

Ariana DeBose becomes the first openly queer woman of colour to win an Oscar for acting.

2021

Quinn, a Canadian soccer player, becomes the first trans and non-binary Olympic gold medallist.

2019

Taiwan becomes the first Asian country to legalise same-sex marriage.

1921

The first UK anti-lesbian legislation is defeated in the House of Lords, on the grounds that making lesbianism illegal will make people want to try it. Hahahahahaha.

1931

Dora Richter becomes the first transgender woman to undergo vaginoplasty (a surgical procedure to remove the penis and create a vagina and vulva).

1936

British athletics champion Mark Weston, who was assigned female at birth, transitions to male, and undergoes surgery in London.

1944

Michael Dillon, a British doctor, author and rower, becomes the first person to have his birth certificate changed from female to male.

1965

The first official gay protest takes place outside the White House in Washington DC.

1970

Wendy Carlos becomes the first trans woman to win a Grammy Award (she actually won three).

1993

Denmark becomes the first country to make registered same-sex partnerships legal.

1993

The first Dyke March takes place in Washington DC, attracting around 20,000 lesbians and their allies.

1996

South Africa becomes the first country in the world to introduce legislation prohibiting discrimination based on sexual orientation, something many US states still don't have.

1999

The first Transgender Day of Remembrance takes place, following the 1998 murder of trans women Rita Hester in Boston.

2005

The first LGBT+ History Month takes place in the UK.

2009

In Iceland, Jóhanna Sigurðardóttir becomes the world's first openly lesbian prime minister. Elio Di Rupo becomes the first gay man to hold the same office in Belgium in 2011.

OG Queers

Same-sex desire wasn't born with *Heartstopper*, and gender exploration has been going on since before togas became a thing. Every era is the LGBTQ+ era.

The real 300

The Spartans depicted in the movie *300* were losers. The real-life super-army of 300 soldiers were the Sacred Band of Thebes, a legendary platoon from the fourth century BCE, who remained unbeaten for 40 years. The Sacred Band of Thebes were 150 pairs of gay warrior lovers, revered as much as they were feared. They thrashed Sparta (told you), but fell at the hands of Alexander the Great and his father, Philip of Macedon, who wept for the 'army of lovers' as he buried them. In 1879, the bones of 254 skeletons, respectfully buried in pairs, were excavated at the site of their fateful last stand at the Greek village of Chaeronea.

Romosexuality?

Ancient Rome was more relaxed about same-sex attraction than some societies but – sense check – they weren't all at it. We believe that some emperors had long-time boyfriends – Nero and Hadrian, for example – but what of the lives of common men and women? The best-preserved Roman town is Pompeii, where the bath house has 16 erotic pictures on the walls; three of which involve gay, bi and lesbian activities, leading us to believe that people weren't offended by them.

Sappho

Sappho of Lesbos (620–570BCE) is basically the patron saint of girls who love girls. The Greek poet isn't just some obscure, distant figure that we as queer people can latch onto. Sappho has always been celebrated as one of the greatest poets that ever lived, with Plato calling her the tenth muse. Thousands of years later, her words of love still resonate.

Elagabalus

From 218–222CE, the Roman Empire was ruled by Elagabalus, the most privileged, powerful, brazenly queer teenager in the world. They were said to wear wigs and make-up and preferred to be addressed as 'my lady'. We don't know if they identified as a woman, but they're the first recorded person in Western history to seek gender-reassignment surgery – they offered half the empire to any physician who could give them a vagina.

Samurai

An elite Japanese military group, Samurai were around from the 1100s until the mid 1800s. Some samurai actively encouraged same-sex relationships, a practice called *wakashūdo*. It's estimated that three per cent of samurai were women – though this may have varied between battles (DNA tests on a 1580 battlefield revealed the number there was around 30 per cent). It doesn't take much of a leap of imagination to assume that if male samurai were partnered up, the women were too.

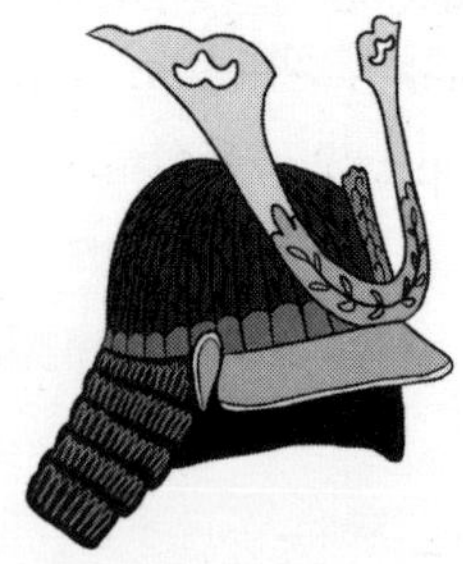

The Kama Sutra

Think it's just a book about sex? Oh no – it's so much more. It's basically a highly influential wellness manual. The ancient Indian text (from around 400CE) is surprisingly non-judgemental about same-sex behaviour and fully acknowledges a third sex. It's particularly refreshing in its discussion of female sexuality. Gay women are named *svairini* and described as 'independent women who frequent their own kind or others' and 'those who refuse husbands'.

Hatshepsut, the first bearded queen

One of Egypt's greatest rulers was Hatshepsut, who ruled from 1473–1458BCE, and is shown wearing a beard in numerous ancient statues. Hatshepsut may have leaned into masculine iconography for its usefulness in making people feel like she was a strong and safe leader – it worked. We can embrace her as a gender-non-conforming role model for the fact that she liked to be called 'his majesty herself'.

Gay manicurists, 2500BCE

Ancient Egypt may also have been home to one of history's first recorded gay couples – Knumhotep and Niankhkhnum. These two were head manicurists (typecasting) to Pharaoh Nyuserre Ini in the 25th century BCE, and were most likely boyfriends. In images, they're positioned together in a way that was usually reserved for husband and wife. They're even buried together, with a romantic picture of them hugging painted in their tomb.

Queer Rulers

Historically, royalty experienced greater freedom than commoners did, which was great news for the titled LGBTQ+s brought up to believe that they could do whatever – and whoever – they wanted.

Princess Isabella of Parma and Maria Christina, Duchess of Teschen

When the pretty Spanish Princess Isabella married the Holy Roman Emperor Joseph II in 1760, she scored big . . . with Joseph's sister, Maria Christina (Mimi). Mimi was beautiful, clever and totally up for some secret girl-on-girl romance. If you're looking for a Disney princess version of gay love, here it is in all its opulent, gaudy, girly glory. Isabella and Mimi were besotted and sent sweet notes to each other all the time, despite living together – of which 200 still survive, some so dreamy and passionate that any reader will swoon on reading them: "I love thee like a madwoman, in a holy way or diabolically, I love you and will love you to the grave."

King James I and the Duke of Buckingham

In 1614, James met 21-year-old squire George Villiers, who was described as 'the handsomest-bodied man in England'. Oh, hello. To say he was the 'favourite' of the king is an understatement. The words in the following love letter from the king to his fave say it all: "I desire only to live in this world for your sake, and that I had rather live banished in any part of the Earth with you than live a sorrowful widow's life without you. And so God bless you, my sweet child and wife, and grant that ye may ever be a comfort to your dear dad and husband."

Queen Nzinga

Warrior Queen Nzinga of Ndongo and Matamba lived in what we now call Angola in the early 1600s – and, boy, was she living. A queen who was a king, she dressed as a man and had many husbands, all of whom dressed as women. Hot. Queen Nzinga fought the Portuguese army in a 30-year war defending her people and territory. She implemented female military leaders and politicians, chose her sister as successor and basically rewrote the rule book on how to rule.

Edward II and Piers Gaveston

The most famous gay king of England is Edward II, who reigned from 1307–1327. In the late 1500s, Shakespeare's mate Christopher Marlowe wrote a play about Edward's life and love for another man. The king's main 'favourite' was Piers Gaveston, the son of a knight. People were suspicious of their relationship, and eventually Edward had to send Gaveston away for his own safety. It didn't end well – Gaveston ended up without his head, and so we have British history's first royal gay tragedy.

Richard the Lionheart

Romantic hero of the Crusades, Richard the Lionheart may have been smooch-buddies with Philip of France. It was said that 'The King of France loved him [Richard] as his own soul' and 'at night the bed did not separate them'. This bed-sharing may have just been political – sharing a bed was the ultimate act of trust, so doing it in front of your courtiers showed the strength of their relationship. But who knows what their reasons really were . . .

Queen Christina of Sweden

The legendary lesbian queen took the throne in 1626, at age six, then abdicated when she was 28 because she couldn't bear the idea of marrying a man. She was highly educated, ambitious and widely travelled, speaking eight languages and voraciously studying anything and everything, from philosophy to painting and sculpture, mathematics to religion. Her 'bedfellow' was the beautiful Countess Ebba Sparre, with whom she shared a long and intimate relationship. There has been speculation that Christina was born with intersex traits, but this may be a way to retroactively explain her wild 'manly' behaviour and adventurous spirit. To paraphrase the Pet Shop Boys: she was never being boring.

Tūtānekai

Takatāpui (rainbow person) is a Māori word to describe people with non-normative gender identities and those who're same-sex-attracted. This inclusive umbrella term (a bit like queer) was chosen by the queer community in the 1980s and 90s to refer to themselves in their own language. The name derives from a story about Māori chief Tūtānekai who mourned having to give up his love for his 'friend' Tiki when he married a woman. Before homophobia was imported from Christian Europe, New Zealand's Māori tribes were thought to be sex positive, open to a multitude of gender identities and romantic possibilities.

Emperor Ai of Han

One of cutest gay stories from history would've made the perfect TikTok. China's Emperor Ai of Han, who ruled from 7–1 BCE, aged just 20, was obviously gay and in love with his political advisor Dong Xian. The story goes that one afternoon after taking a nap together, Ai woke up tangled up with Dong Xian, but rather than disturb him, he cut off his sleeve to wriggle out of bed without waking him. Their love, and queer love in general, is sometimes referred to in Chinese as the Passion of the Cut Sleeve – 断袖之癖 – and that's the gayest name for being gay you could wish for.

Colonialism and LGBTQ+ freedoms

What's the UK's biggest export ever? It might be homophobia . . .

When we talk about the UK's colonial past, we're talking about colonising other countries. Which means barging into a place with its own culture and beliefs and making the people that live there do as we say, which is pretty horrific. The main goal of colonisers was usually to gain access to valuable goods, such as gold, rubber or cocoa. In the process, they stole land, labour and resources, erased indigenous cultures and committed unspeakable acts of violence.

These parts of colonial history alone are unforgivable – but one of the unforeseen legacies of colonialism that people rarely talk about is the spread of homophobia and transphobia around the world. Before colonisers showed up and brought homophobic attitudes into the colonial governments and cultures they created, dozens of countries had their own, more tolerant ways of seeing queerness. Often, they saw it as a normal part of life – head to page 102 to read about cultures that have embraced queerness over time.

Europe's conquering era in the 1700s and 1800s also coincided with its peak Christian era. When Europeans turned up in Africa, Asia, the Americas and Australia, they brought religion with them. Many missionaries preached a puritanical version of Christianity that very much condemned same-sex relationships, and frowned upon non-traditional gender expression.

Most colonised countries have gradually returned to independence over time – but do you know what they can't get back? Their original systems of belief. When colonising countries such as the UK took control of places, they rewrote the laws, and while most conquering European nations have overturned their backward anti-LGBTQ+ legislation, the countries they colonised often have not.

One of the most damaging exports was a law called Section 377. Created in Britain in 1862, and subsequently exported across the empire, it condemned 'whoever voluntarily has carnal intercourse against the order of nature with any man, woman or animal'. The law is still in force in places like Pakistan, Bangladesh, Singapore and Malaysia, meaning millions are still living with this imported legacy of hatred.

It's not all doom and gloom though; change can happen. In 2018, India overturned Section 377, freeing 1.4 billion people from 150 years of oppression.

Vive la Gender Révolution!

So many gender-non-conforming trailblazers were French. Could France be the queerest country? *Oui, probablement!*

The transgender musketeer

The Chevalier d'Eon was born in 1728 to an aristocratic family with no money. They were smart, studied law and, in 1756, began an astonishing career that included spying for King Louis XV, infiltrating the Russian court by assuming the identity of a woman, and being a swashbuckling military captain and a diplomatic ambassador in London. Eventually, in 1777, they set up house back in France and began living life as a woman.

Such was the fame of the Chevalier that bookmakers started to take bets as to whether they were male or female. The Chevalier understandably refused to accept a humiliating examination and speculation raged on. When the French Revolution began in 1789, their income was suspended, so they took to performing in fencing tournaments in full female attire, further adding to their celebrity. After a nasty injury in 1796, things began to wind down for the Chevalier, and they died in London at the ripe old age of 81. Their grave is lost, but you can visit the memorial of Europe's first openly trans icon at St Pancras Old Church in London.

The romantic feminist

George Sand was one of France's leading and prolific writers of the 19th century, writing 70 (!!!) novels. Although you might've taken her for a man – what with the trousers and tobacco-smoking (both against the law for a woman at the time) – George was indeed a woman, a passionate female libertine. Sand married a man at 18, but after some years, entered a 'romantic rebellion', having affairs with many men and – *bonjour madame* – a woman, Marie Dorval, a famous actress who completely ignored the pleas of a former lover to stay away from George.

The Sun King's queer spare

France's most famous King, Louis XIV, had a baby brother, Philippe I, Duke of Orléans (1640–1701), who was essentially brought up as a girl, so as not to give him any funny ideas about who was top *chien*. Philippe was *pas de* bothered, and fully embraced his feminine side. The charismatic duke lived a queer fairytale life: marrying, having children, taking male lovers, dressing as a shepherdess and leading armies to victory in battle. He was popular with the people, and no one killed him or persecuted him. *Fin*.

Queer Gods and Saints

Queerness and religion haven't always been easy bedfellows, but it's hard to deny the divine power of love. Here are a few of the top LGBTQ+ icons and stories from religion and religious life.

Lord Shiva and Lord Vishnu (as Mohini)

Gods have a long history of shape-shifting. Hindu legends aren't messing around when they tell the story of the great god Shiva being seduced by the supreme god Vishnu, in the form of the beautiful maiden Mohini. These two deities, some of the most revered in Hinduism, even have a child together, called Sastha. Talk about messy relationship.

Hermaphroditus

We don't use the term hermaphrodite (see page 17) nowadays when talking about human biology, because it carries a sexual charge and objectifies people. But the god Hermaphroditus themself is fascinating. According to Greek myth, Hermaphroditus was the child of gods Aphrodite and Hermes. At age 15, Hermaphroditus met a nymph called Salmacis, who was swimming in her pool. Salmacis became instantly besotted, begging the gods to join them together for ever, which they did, merging them in one single body. That is one of the ways the ancient Greeks explained intersex, trans or even gay people – we took a dip in the waters of Salmacis.

Saint Wilgefortis (the female Christ)

Yes, there's a trans saint! If you see a depiction of Jesus on a cross in a dress, you're likely actually looking at Wilgefortis. The legend goes that Portugese Princess Wilgefortis (meaning 'courageous virgin') refused to marry a man and asked God to help her out and make her hideous. Ta-da! By some miracle, they grew a beard, enough to put off undesirable male suitors. Trigger/patriarchy warning: their dad had them crucified and they had their sainthood revoked in 1969 by the Catholic church. History gives. History takes away.

Jonathan and David: the Bible's greatest love story

David slew the giant Goliath in the Bible. You probably know that bit. But did you know that David's relationship with his 'friend' Jonathan has been held up for centuries as the ideal love between men? Serious biblical scholars debate it, and queer people of faith look to Jonathan and David as proof that Christianity approves of same-sex unions. Their relationship is given more space than any other in scripture, and their love is so deep that at times the words prickle with romance: "Your love for me was wonderful, surpassing the love of women," David said of Jonathan. Swoon.

Tu'er Shen the rabbit god

The Chinese protector of the LGBTQ+ community is a rabbit god called Tu'er Shen. The god appears in 17th and 18th century folk tales and in 2023, the first temple to Tu'er Shen was erected in Taipei, Taiwan.

Bisexual Buccaneers and Lesbians Ahoy!

Depictions of pirates in popular culture are often a bit camp, but is there more to it than a nice frock coat and a smudge of eyeliner?

Oooh arrrr! Gender-fluid pirates

Navies around the world were not massive fans of admitting women – but pirates were not fans of rules, so would sometimes allow female crew members, if they lived as men on board. Whether this was a draw for people that we'd identify as trans or non-binary today, or just a part of 'the job', we'll never know. **Anne Bonny** and **Mary Read** were two such women. Both began dressing as boys at a young age – Anne was called Andy; Mary was known as Mark. Anne began a relationship with notorious pirate Jack Rackham, but there are reports that she was attracted to Mary, while dressed as a man.

These two fearless women were said to fight harder and meaner than their male crewmates, pistol in one hand, cutlass in the other.

Matelotage: gay marriage for the pirates of the Caribbean

Buccaneers were the pirates of the Caribbean – except legal. In the 1600s and 1700s, the British government gave them permission to rob the Spanish, as long as they shared the booty. Some of them would team up in a form of same-sex marriage called 'matelotage'. This was an official ceremony in which they would exchange rings and promise to leave all their worldly goods to each other. Pretty intense. Some matelots were probably just best friends, but others were definitely lovers, like Robert Culliford, who ran away with his 'great consort', John Swann, in 1698.

Interracial teenage love

In a lot of ways, pirates aren't the greatest role models, but making up your own moral code has its advantages. It wasn't only gays and women that were afforded benefits they mightn't have had as landlubbers – records show that white pirates 'married' Black pirates, as in the case of **Richard Baker** and **Olaudah Equiano**. The two were said to have fallen in love as teenagers while living at sea. For two years, they had a matelotage situation and were 'inseparable', sharing a bed and spending nights 'lain in each other's bosoms'.

Cowboys and Gilded Age Girls

America: the land of the free – but not for everyone, obviously.

Can't marry? Adopt!

Revolutionary gay war hero **Baron von Steuben** served under George Washington from 1778. He was a brave and effective leader, instrumental in winning the American Revolutionary War against the British. During the war, he lived with his aides-de-camp, William North and Benjamin Walker, who were likely in a relationship. After the war, von Steuben adopted them as his sons as a way to become family – a sort of loophole gay marriage – and all three lived together, with the two younger men later inheriting his estate.

ASSUMPTION SMASH

The Wild West was straight as an arrow

Western films are the archetypal macho entertainment, but the Wild West was probably wilder than we've been told. Take **One-Eyed Charlie**, one of the most notorious stagecoach drivers in the Old West. Upon his death in 1879, it was discovered that Charlie was in fact born Charlotte. Today, the cowboy way of life is embraced by the LGBTQ+ community. Gay rodeos began in the 1970s and became an official thing in 1985, with the arrival of the International Gay Rodeo Association.

Donut riot (no, do)

The first queer uprising in the US is often attributed to the Cooper Do-nuts Riot in Los Angeles, which took place in May 1959, ten years before Stonewall. Cooper Do-nuts was next to two gay bars and was popular with after-hours LGBTQ+ patrons. One night when five customers, including two drag queens, were arrested, customers started throwing coffee and doughnuts in protest. More police arrived on the scene, blocking off the street, and beating up and arresting more people. Official records of the incident are missing or have been destroyed.

Boston Marriage

First used in 1893, this term for a loving, long-lasting relationship between two women takes its name from the city of Boston, Massachusetts, on the east coast of the US. Some of these partnerships we might not consider gay – others probably were. Why Boston? Because this was a part of the US where there was a higher number of educated, middle and upper-class women, who did not have to marry to feel financially stable. They could live with each other instead. More tea, Lavinia?

War Heroes

War, what is it good for? Stories of exceptional bravery and yellow-bellied skullduggery.

Lesbian action hero on wheels

If you're looking for a queer war hero, you've found her. **Toupie Lowther** (1874–1944) was one hell of an adventurous lesbian. She was a talented sportswoman who played professional tennis but also excelled in fencing, ju-jitsu and weight-lifting. When WWI broke out, she leapt into the fray, forming an all-female ambulance crew to rescue injured soldiers from the French front line, braving shellfire, gas and bombs. After the war, Toupie received medals from the British and the French, and inspired Radclyffe Hall's seminal lesbian novel *The Well of Loneliness*. Her ambulance unit is regarded as a pretty much lesbian endeavour and absolutely needs to be made into a film.

The gay MPs who stood against Hitler

The Glamour Boys was a name given to a group of British MPs who warned about the evils of Hitler and Nazism from as early as 1932 and were ignored. As you might guess, the name 'Glamour Boys' was a slur. Incredibly, it was given to them by the then prime minister Neville Chamberlain, who sought to undermine the opinions of these men, most of whom were gay or bisexual, by using their sexuality against them. The group of ten men included Bob Bernays, Ronnie Cartland, Victor Cazalet and Jack Macnamara – all of whom were killed in action during WWII.

The quiet geek who won the war

It's hard to overstate the importance of **Alan Turing's** contribution to the war effort in WWII. With his team at Bletchley Park, the genius mathematician and father of computing cracked the Nazi 'Enigma' code with a machine Turing had invented. This meant the British could decode and read Nazi messages. In doing so, it's believed that he shortened the war by between two and four years, saving an estimated 14–21 million lives. Despite this, seven years after the war ended, Turing was arrested for being gay, given a hormone therapy sometimes referred to as 'chemical castration', and was banned from working in the government. Shit, people can be cruel. Two years later, in 1954, he killed himself. In 2013, the Queen 'pardoned' Turing, and in 2021, he was put on the UK's most valuable currency, the £50 note.

fluid figures

Not gay-gay, not straight-straight, some historical figures might fall somewhere in the middle . . .

When we look at the history books, it's clear that many people we assume to be straight, a dead-cert zero on the Kinsey scale, are actually more complicated. Why should we care? Because people in power have the capacity to take away LGBTQ+ rights, and if they're secretly one of us, that's hypocrisy. When we're 'othered' by those in power, we can direct their attention to a who's who of their heroes and say, well, this bunch were a bit queer too.

Eleanor Roosevelt

When her husband, President Franklin D. Roosevelt, took a mistress, the US's First Lady decided to take one too. Eleanor Roosevelt's lady-love wasn't just a casual hook-up. Her intense and lasting relationship with journalist Lorena Hickok,

'Hick', is documented in the 3,000 letters they sent to each other. Excerpt: "I want to put my arms around you and kiss you at the corner of your mouth."

Alexander Hamilton

If you've seen the Broadway show, you'll know that US Founding Father Alexander Hamilton signed the US constitution but not that he had a ridiculously flirtatious friendship with George Washington's aide John Laurens, writing: "I wish, my Dear Laurens, it were in my power, by actions rather than words, to convince you that I love you." What actions might those be, eh?

Sigmund Freud

The father of psychiatry believed all adults were bisexual to some degree and he himself may have had a love affair with a fellow doctor, Wilhelm Fliess, with whom he regularly went away with for 'congresses'. He wrote to Fliess in 1898: "I do not in the least underestimate bisexuality . . . I expect it to provide all further enlightenment."

Winston Churchill

Wartime prime minister Winston Churchill once admitted to shagging beautiful matinée idol Ivor Novello, just to see what it was like. He described the experience as 'very musical'. But despite this, he was no ally. In 1954, after the arrests of multiple high-profile men for homosexual offences, the government discussed making laws more lenient – but Churchill flat out refused. Oh, hello, Hypocrisy, your ears must be burning.

Places That Recognise More Than Two Genders

Life is a miracle. Your existence on a small blue planet in a vast universe is madly improbable, but, amazingly, you're here. Each of us takes a different path – and we all deserve to be happy. Cultures around the world have known this since the dawn of time – and because trans and non-binary people have always existed, most societies have a rich history of non-normative gender expression.

INDIA AND PAKISTAN

The 'third-sex' **Hijra** of South Asia have been recorded for thousands of years, and communities still flourish today. The Hijra, far from being persecuted, rose to prominent positions of power under both Hindu and Islamic leaders. Hijra have legal rights as a third sex in countries including Bangladesh, India and Pakistan, and they have sacred roles, performing as part of marriage and birth ceremonies. They even have powers to curse individuals who are disrespectful. The original superheroes, then.

MEXICO

In the Oaxaca region of Mexico, the **Muxe** is a person who was born male but doesn't exhibit traditional masculine behaviours. Muxes are sometimes seen as a blessing to a family because they traditionally are more likely to help out around the home and look after their mothers. If a 'straight' man has a romantic moment with a Muxe, he isn't seen as gay. Oh, and Muxes can identify as straight, gay, bi or asexual.

VIKING SCANDINAVIA

Archaeologists have discovered ancient graves in Northern Europe where skeletons of one sex are buried with the trappings of the opposite gender, including males in dresses and brooches normally associated with females. The skeletons of women are sometimes found with weapons associated with men, suggesting that some women forged a path beyond traditional gender roles. One burial site found in 1878 contained a particularly high-status Viking warrior, and in 2011, scientists realised that this warrior was a woman. This person may have been trans or non-binary – or not. All we can say is that notions of cis masculine supremacy aren't as uniform as we're led to believe.

PERSIA

Discoveries of 3,000-year-old Persian graves in modern-day Iran suggests that gender wasn't a binary affair in this ancient civilisation. Most excavated graves were discovered soley with items thought to be signifiers of one particular sex, male or female, but around 20 per cent were found to contain a mixture of 'male' *and* 'female' objects. This careful burial act shows us that the culture not only recognised but respected some version of gender variance.

NORTH AMERICA

Native American culture celebrates the spiritual gifts of each individual, and individuals with both masculine and feminine qualities are celebrated for having the gifts of both men and women. These individuals are held in high esteem, often selected as spiritual leaders. Native Americans focus on people's spirit, rather than seeing them as a rigid set of gendered flesh-bags. It's also worth remembering that people with fluid gender expression aren't restricted by gender roles – which makes them very useful to have around. Again, superheroes.

THAILAND

In Thailand, **Kathoeys** are seen as a third sex combining the souls of men and women in one body. It's not all good news though. Trans women in Thailand cannot legally change their sex, and gender non-conformity is widely seen as a punishment for misdeeds in a past life. Ahhh, crap!

PACIFIC ISLANDS

When Sasha Colby won US *Drag Race* season 15, she taught us about the **Mahu**: Hawaiian and Tahitian gender-non-conforming people. Traditionally, Mahu are teachers, protectors of cultural traditions and practitioners of dance and song, often taking on the role of a goddess – which totally tracks with Sasha. In 1789, the Mahu were recorded in the logbook of Captain Bligh (the naval officer in command during the infamous mutiny on the *Bounty*). He wrote: "A class of people very common . . . although I was certain [he] was a man, [he] had great marks of effeminacy about him." When the French post-impressionist painter Paul Gaugin, whose paintings sell for over £100 million today, moved to Tahiti, he was viewed as a Mahu because of his long hair and flamboyant manner.

Worldwide Pride

Being queer is a very different experience depending on where you live in the world. Here are just a few facts and stats from countries that are making strides in equality and acceptance – and some that are doing the opposite.

Swede smell of equality

In 1972, Sweden became the first country to permit people who were transgender to legally change their sex, while providing free gender-reassignment surgery.

Trans America

A 2023 Pew Research Center study found that one in 20 Americans under 30 identifies as transgender or non-binary (two per cent identify as trans and three per cent as non-binary). But life for trans people in the USA is getting harder. In 2022, 155 anti-trans bills were filed in the US.

Pride in São Paulo

Pride marches around the world can be massive. Between three and five million people attend São Paulo Pride every year, one of the largest gatherings on the planet. São Paulo holds the Guinness World Record for the biggest Pride festival, injecting approximately $100 million into the city's economy yearly.

Naurrr way! Saurrr noice!

Australian women's soccer is smashing queer representation firmly into the back of the net. When the squad (lovingly dubbed 'The Matildas' after Australian song 'Waltzing Matilda') took part in the 2023 World Cup, nine of the first-team players plus three reserves were in same-sex relationships. Can you imagine that happening in men's football? All but two being queer? The answer is surely 'naur!'.

Pole dancers

Every continent in the world has hosted a Pride festival – even chilly Antarctica, which held its first Pride event in 2018, proving the 'we're everywhere' point beautifully – with penguins.

Generation fabulous

The award for queerest generation goes to . . . Gen Z! According to a 2023 Ipsos global poll, 18 per cent of those born between 1997 and 2003 identify as LGBTQ+. That's almost one in five (versus ten per cent of Millenials and nine per cent of the global population as a whole).

Out in Africa

Being LGBTQ+ is legal in just 22 of Africa's 54 countries. Some countries that have changed their laws in favour of LGBTQ+ rights recently are Angola (in 2019), Botswana (in 2019) and Mozambique (in 2015). Others have taken a step back – in 2023 Uganda made it illegal to identify as LGBTQ+.

A Tale of Three Cities

The number of queer people living in England and Wales is equal to the combined populations of Liverpool, Manchester and Cardiff combined. Incidentally, three incredibly welcoming cities for the LGBTQ+ community!

Queered-up Culture

We Need to See It, to Be It

We've never had so much LGBTQ+ representation as today – but more of something can only be good (if it's actually good). As queer kids, when we see ourselves onscreen it allows us to picture our future – like a zero-stakes rehearsal of how to cope in the world. This is especially important for those of us trapped in the closet, dreaming of a day we can live authentically. So, authentic voices, characters, actors and writing are all the more important. It doesn't necessarily have to come from lived experience (though this obviously is a big bonus, in terms of content and representation) – some amazing books about gay male love are written by women; some great gay films are directed by straight men. They just need specificity and truth.

It's also important that LGBTQ+ storylines make it into the mainstream, in things that everyone is watching, reading or consuming. (*Heartstopper* isn't attracting groups of heterosexual bros.) But this can be at the expense of showing the diverse experiences of the whole LGBTQ+ community. When we do get mainstream representation, 90 per cent of the time it's watered down to be palatable to all audiences, and becomes a bit samey. Most queer success stories in mainstream culture are cosy and heart-warming, or resort to stereotypes like the funny or fashionable gay (these stereotypes are one of the evils that can come through representation, however well-intentioned). Tragic storylines, where we're portrayed as a victim are common, as is a focus on romance and sex. Straight audiences don't subsist on a restricted diet of rom coms, so why should we? True, no one story can represent everyone. But, by the same token, there should be a bit of variation in mainstream culture, and young LGBTQ+ people should be able to see themselves somewhere.

My favourite *Drag Race* podcast, *Alright Mary*, calls the most reliable queens of *Drag Race*, the ones they love no matter how crap they look or badly they perform in the challenges, 'Pizza Queens', because they love pizza and even bad pizza is pretty great. That's what I'm looking for with queer media representation: sloppy, messy, delicious, moreish pizza – Hannah Einbinder in *Hacks*, Thomas in *Downton Abbey*, Anne Lister in *Gentleman Jack*, Villanelle in *Killing Eve*, Titus Andromedon from *The Unbreakable Kimmy Schmidt*. Like this lot, we're all a glorious mix of fantastic and infuriating.

So, find a cosy corner and let's dive into queer culture – from the big screen to music, theatre, fashion and beyond.

A–Z of Camp

What is camp? Who is it? Why do we love it and why do we hate it?

Camp is an over-the-top presentation that doesn't take itself too seriously. OR takes itself FAR TOO seriously. When something is so big as to be unreal or unbelievable, it slips into camp, and the absurdity makes us laugh. The queer community loves a bit of camp because it's acting with a capital A, something a lot of us start doing when we're little kids. Sometimes it's intentional, like Jennifer Coolidge doing sexy faces and wiggling about. Sometimes it's by accident, like Faye Dunaway in *Mommie Dearest*, where her 'serious' performance is too HUGE not to be hilarious.

Camp can be bitchy. It can be cute. It can be fabulous and it can also be predictable. It can be a manner of speech, an outfit, a bedspread – almost anything. What camp are you in when it comes to camp? Have a read-through of this A–Z and pick your faves . . .

ASSUMPTION SMASH

Lesbians aren't camp

Instagram account Butchcamp, run by Isabella Toledo and Rosie Eveleigh, says they absolutely are. Their calendars, featuring queer girl moments of campness such as 'Patricia Highsmith smuggling pet snails across borders in her bra', are nothing short of inspired.

A is for . . . Alan Carr's voice
B is for . . . *Batman* (1960s)
C is for . . . Charity Shop Sue
D is for . . . Double-barrelled drag names, e.g. Angeria Paris VanMicheals
E is for . . . Eurovision
F is for . . . Flamingos
G is for . . . *Glee* covers
H is for . . . *High School Musical*
I is for . . . 'I Want to Break Free' MV by Queen
J is for . . . Judy Garland movies
K is for . . . Katy Perry's hamburger dress
L is for . . . Leslie Jordan
M is for . . . *M3GAN*
N is for . . . Net curtains
O is for . . . Oscar Wilde plays
P is for . . . Pop socks
Q is for . . . *Queer Eye*'s Jonathan van Ness
R is for . . . RuPaul in 'But I'm a Cheerleader'
S is for . . . *Sharknado*
T is for . . . Tinky-Winky
U is for . . . Ursula the Sea Witch
V is for . . . Victoria Scone
W is for . . . *What We Do in the Shadows*
X is for . . . *Xena: Warrior Princess*
Y is for . . . the YMCA dance
Z is for . . . Zebras (camp horses)

Fashion: We Invented That

Fashion is a wonderful and complicated business that's almost impossible to keep up with. There are, however, a few essential and iconic fashion looks that every LGBTQ+er should know – game-changing signature moments and movements that are constantly being referenced, reinvented and re-worn by our community. Which do you love? Which do you hate? Which will you copy?

1930s

Marlene Dietrich

Top hat and tails plus full glam face

1940s

Joan Crawford

Victory rolls hair, bitch pout, shoulders the size of a sofa

1950s

Bette Davis

Shoulder-baring gown with a brooch, occasional eye-patch

Marilyn Monroe

Floor-length fuchsia tube dress with matching gloves

1960s

Audrey Hepburn

LBD (little black dress), up-do, tiara, croissant and coffee

Twiggy

Shift dress, side part, nude lip, drawn-on spider lashes

1970s

Tina Turner and Cher

Bob Mackie gold and red glittery fringe dress

Vivienne Westwood

Asymmetric hemlines, tartan and safety pins

1980s

Grace Jones

Hooded dress on a flat-top haircut

Goths

Black everything, thick eyeliner, dark lips

1990s

Linda Evangelista and Naomi Campbell

Cropped hair, Versace dresses, dramatic neutrals make-up

Geri Halliwell

Union Jack tea-towel dress, stripey orange hair

2000s

Mean Girls

Pink sweaters, slogan tank tops and short skirts

2010s

Red-carpet Rihanna

Pope. Omelette. Crystal-encrusted flapper. Wine glass

2020s

Barbie

Pink cowboy or gingham dress. Sharpie face scribbles

Wednesday & M3GAN

Dark Academia aesthetics: Peter Pan collar, stripes, bows, boots

LGBTQ+ designers to search

Nearly every legendary fashion designer you can think of was, or is, queer. Why? Perhaps because it's one of the few careers where it's 'acceptable' to luxuriate in femininity without condemnation. Here are a few of the big names: Christian Dior, Cristóbal Balenciaga, Yves Saint Laurent, Gianni Versace, Alexander McQueen, Tom Ford, Marc Jacobs, Patricia Field, Kenzō Takada, Christopher Kane, Alessandro Michele, Nicolas Ghesquière, Olivier Rousteing, Harris Reed.

Seven fashion references every homo should know (plus one no-no)

1983 – Katharine Hamnett, slogan tees
1986 – Alaïa, hooded dress
1990 – Jean Paul Gaultier, cone bra corset
1992 – Mugler, motorcycle bustier
1994 – Westwood, plaid dress
2005 – Viktor & Rolf, pillow and quilt dress
2019 – Iris van Herpen, hypnosis dresses

Don't try this at home . . .
1996 – Alexander McQueen, bumsters

Androgyny in the 80s

The fashion for blurring gender really got going in the early 1980s, when subverting norms and playing dress-up was part of the pop-star package.

Pop stars have played with gender since Little Richard invented the game in the 1950s, but something special happened in the 80s. Kids raised on the push-pull of glam rock (femme) and punk (masc) were ready to make a splash with a fearless attitude and love of pop theatrics. Here are the era's key players . . .

Klaus Nomi

A half-clown, half-alien performance artist with a voice as high as the heavens and PVC power-shoulders. Nomi backed up Bowie on *Saturday Night Live* in 1979 and that alone puts him in the queer pantheon.

Sylvester

'When You Make Me Feel (Mighty Real)' was released in 1978, it was an instant queer anthem. Sylvester identified as a gay man, and his gender presentation was as fluid and femme as his unmistakable falsetto.

Grace Jones

The queen of masculinity. The suit and flat-top on the cover of her 1981 album *Nightclubbing* took her to icon status.

Duran Duran

With their love of bows, lip gloss, and peach and plum hair dye, Nick Rhodes and John Taylor could well be the blueprint for K-Pop idols like Jeonghan (Seventeen), Yeonjun (TXT) or even V from BTS.

Boy George

George was a goddess of a gay man with a soulful voice, swishing around in clothes that weren't for girls but weren't for boys either.

Annie Lennox

Eurythmics' Annie Lennox was – and still is – stunning, but she didn't rest on pretty. If her cropped tangerine hair and men's suits scared your grandpa, the promo for 'Who's That Girl' (1983) – where Lennox dragged up as a man, complete with fake sideburns – would have finished him off.

Freddie Mercury

The video to Queen's 'I Want to Break Free' (1984), where the band dressed in drag, sent America into meltdown. They could not handle tashed-up Freddie in stockings and PVC mini-skirt doing a light spring clean.

Prince

Most British 'gender-benders' weren't that sexy. Prince was hot as hell in high heels, a trench coat and not much else. His fashion sense was so fluid that he only had to wear a blouse and media speculation about his sexuality would pop off! Something still going on with artists like Harry Styles.

Queer Art Timeline

Queer people are really good at making art, depicting unique points of view that can be as surprising and challenging as they are beautiful.

1914

Surreal artist Claude Cahun meets Marcel Moore (not their 'given names') and the two arguably gender-queer women become lifelong partners in art and romance.

1877

Walter Crane paints the *Renaissance of Venus*, using a male model because his wife forbade female models in the house: Welcome, an accidental trans beauty.

1864

Simeon Solomon – the gay, Jewish Pre-Raphaelite – paints lesbian icon Sappho and her lover, Erinna, now displayed at Tate Britain.

1916

Bloomsbury Group couple Duncan Grant and Vanessa Bell move to Charleston in East Sussex, the queerest, artiest house in the entire country.

1929

Polish bisexual superstar of art deco Tamara de Lempicka paints her masterwork, *Autoportrait* (*Tamara in a Green Bugati.*)

1930s–40s

Lesbian cabaret star Suzy Solidor sets out to becom[e] the most painted woman i[n] the world, commissioning 250 portraits (selfies?) from the likes of Picasso and Man Ray.

2022

Trans teen Victor Langlois (FEWOCiOUS) sells nearly $20 million worth of his art in 24 hours.

2021

Kehinde Wiley, a Black gay painter from LA, has his first solo National Gallery show in London, reimagining Romantic old masters with Black protagonists.

2018

Charlotte Prodger wins the Turner Prize with a film exploring queerness and gender identity, *BRIDGIT*, shot on an iPhone.

100BCE

The OG bi-guy Alexander the Great is depicted in a mosaic at Pompeii, black hair flowing, in a shining suit of armour with a Medusa breastplate like a Balmain-Versace collab.

1440

The sculptor Donatello is the first 'openly gay' artist at a time when he could be burned at the stake for it.

1484

Botticelli paints *The Birth of Venus* for the mega-rich Medici family. Botticelli may have been gay or bisexual – he was accused of sodomy in 1502, but the charge was dropped.

1503

Leonardo da Vinci paints the *Mona Lisa*. Like Botticelli, another Renaissance artist, Leonardo is arrested and brought before the anti-gay court or 'Office of the Night'.

1620

Celebrated Baroque sculptor Bernini carves a marble mattress for the recently discovered ancient Roman statue of the androgynous god Hermaphroditus to sleep on. The sculpture is now in the Louvre, in Paris.

1822

Rosa Bonheur, the first celebrated openly lesbian painter, is born in Bordeaux. Bonheur is famed for acquiring a license from the police to dress like a male peasant. So on trend.

1939

Bisexual Mexican artist Frida Kahlo paints *The Two Fridas* after her divorce from Diego Rivera.

1942

Gluck works on her/their/his confrontational wartime self-portrait. Androgynous name, gender-non-conforming, defiantly queer – Gluck would fit in brilliantly today.

1944

Gay artillery officer Anthony Clarke disobeys orders to destroy the town of Sansepolcro in Italy in order to save Piero della Francesca's *The Resurrection*.

1963

David Hockney exhibits *Domestic Scene, Los Angeles*, a suggestive and comical picture with one nude man in an apron washing another in a bucket.

1981

Jean-Michel Basquiat's first show takes place alongside a plethora of queer artists, but the Black bisexual artist is the one who makes the most waves.

2010

The most expensive painting by a living artist sells for $110 million: a US flag by gay painter Jasper Johns.

Disney Villains: Are They a Bit, You Know?

There are two types of *Little Mermaid* fans in this world: those who want to dress up as Ariel, and those who want to dress up as Ursula. For me, it's the octopus every time.

Queer people often have a soft spot for the villains. In a world of dimwits, there's something reassuring about a clever-clogs villain who has a plan and puts in the hard work. You have to respect them. You also have to laugh at them, because they're camp as hell and they always fail. LOL. No wonder Captain Hook, Jafar, Scar, Shere Khan and Anton Ego are such bitter old queens, with such relatable eye-rolls – they resent the hope and youthful optimism of the hero.

Disney's female villains are just as queer-coded, having a draggy, larger-than-life quality. The Wicked Queen in *Snow White* was based on the surly beauty of Joan Crawford. Fan-favourite Ursula from *The Little Mermaid* was inspired by pioneering drag performer Divine, while Yzma from *The Emperor's New Groove* was voiced by bona fide gay icon Eartha Kitt. Cruella de Vil might not seem very gay – but did you know her inspiration came from the wild, untameable actress Tallulah Bankhead?

And that's before we even get to Gaston and *Beauty and the Beast* – how many straight men sing about interior design?! We can totally read Gaston as queer. His body isn't just gym-toned, he's beyond buff and he wants us to know it, ripping his shirt open to show off his wares. LaFou is obsessed, and who can blame him? And it doesn't end there. Don't sue me, but Cogsworth and Lumière are dating. Cogsworth is jealous because Lumière is a bi guy running around dripping wax all over the palace, carrying on with feather dusters and whatnot. Just a theory.

Reclaiming villainy

Hollywood has a history of making the villain queer. That's horribly prejudiced – but it secretly feels badass. As teenagers, a lot of LGBTQ+ kids feel powerless, so seeing a queer boss-witch owning everyone is exhilarating, even if they do get killed off. Naturally, we dream of being the good guy and getting the happy ending we deserve – but spoiling everything and crushing dreams is a great back-up option.

The father of 'gay' Disney

Brace yourself for the full tea: the supervising animator behind Jafar, Scar and Gaston – not to mention OG Disney daddy King Triton and hunky Hercules – is a gay man. Andreas Deja started working at Disney in the mid 80s and was there all through Disney's 90s renaissance and beyond, doing a fantastic job of creating iconic characters that we will never stop loving.

Adorably Queer

It's not only Disney that's giving. Many of our cute favourites have secret LGBTQ+ backstories.

The 'trans' Care Bear

Queer people love finding new representation, especially when it's as wholesome as this. **Funshine Bear** started out as a female character, voiced in 80s cartoons by female actors. But when the franchise relaunched in the 2000s, the bear had become male and was voiced by men. Therefore, if we care to, we can see the cuddly yellow furball as trans masc. And I very much do.

The 'gay' Muppets

Debate rages on about if Bert and Ernie are BFs or just BFFs, but we can surely agree that **Bunsen** and **Beaker** are gay for each other, after numerous hints about their laboratory romance over the years. If that's not enough, Scooter was voiced by gay puppeteer Richard Hunt from 1976 to 1992, who infused him with his own personality and voice. Hunt sadly died of an AIDS-related illness and was described by Mark Hamill (who played Luke Skywalker) as "one of the best friends my family ever has ever had".

The 'non-binary' lazy egg

Gudetama is the breakout Sanrio star giving Hello Kitty a run for her no-mouth money. Their name literally means 'lazy egg' and they capture the 'can't be arsed' millennial malaise perfectly. Since Gude is an unfertilised egg, the angst-ridden layabout obviously goes by they/them pronouns. (Well, it's 'headcanon' in my house.)

The 'intersex' Pokémon

Meowth is the only Pokémon that can hold a decent conversation – apologies to Psyduck. Meowth was voiced by trans voice actor Maddie Blaustein, who was born intersex but assigned male at birth. She played sassy kitty Meowth from 1997–2005 in ten movies and nearly 400 episodes of the Pokémon animé series.

Playmobil™ makes myth reality

Anyone who's read Madeline Miller's Orange-Prize-winning novel *The Song of Achilles* knows that the ancient Greek heroes Achilles and Patroclus are the OG (fictional?) gay couple. If straight men are obsessed with the Roman Empire, gay men are nuts for Greek myths, so, lucky for us, in 2020 Playmobil™ released an Achilles and Patroclus playset, complete with chariot.

LGBTQ+ Sporting Timeline

Some of us use words, music or clothes to express ourselves. Some of us find our tribe on the sports pitch. Here are some key LGBTQ+ milestones . . .

1981
Tennis star Billie Jean King is forced out of the closet, becoming the most visible face of LGBTQ+ sports.

1982
The first Gay Games takes place in San Francisco.

1990
Justin Fashanu, the first Black footballer to get a £1 million transfer fee is dragged out of the closet, making him the first professional footballer to be out while still playing.

1991
Stonewall FC, the UK's first gay football club, forms in London.

1998
One of the world's greatest golfers, Patty Sheehan, comes out as a lesbian.

2005
WNBA player Sheryl Swoopes is one of the first African-American athletes to come out.

2021
Carl Nassib is the first active NFL player to come out as gay.

2022
Jake Daniels comes out as gay, aged 17, becoming the UK's only male professional footballer to be publicly out, and the first since Justin Fashanu in 1990.

2023
Trans powerlifter JayCee Cooper wins a legal battle against USA Powerlifting after they banned her from competing in women's competitions.

1905

Lily Parr, a football great who is said to have scored 900 goals in her day, is born. Her team draw a crowd of 53,000 to their Boxing Day game at Goodison Park in 1920.

1926

Tattooed gender-non-conforming Betty 'Joe' Carstairs becomes the fastest woman on water, winning the Duke of York's trophy for power boating. She also wins the heart of Marlene Dietrich.

1928

British athletics star Mark Weston is born. Diagnosed with Differences of Sexual Development, he seeks gender-affirming surgery aged 31, becoming Mark and getting married in the same year.

1938

German high jumper Dora Ratjen is arrested and removed from competitive sports when they're discovered to have intersex characteristics.

1971

Mike Beuttler, the first openly gay Formula One racing driver, makes his debut at Silverstone.

1976

British figure skater John Curry wins gold at the Olympic Games, is outed as gay by a German newspaper and wins the World Championship title – in that order.

2009

Gareth Thomas, the Welsh team's most capped Rugby player, comes out.

2012

Record-breaking lesbian boxer Nicola Adams wins gold at the London Olympic Games.

2012

Tom Daley wins the first of his four Olympic medals – more than any other British diver.

2019

India's fastest sprinter Dutee Chand reveals that she's in a relationship with another woman.

Keeping It Real

Looking for diverse and interesting queer representation on TV? Time for a reality check.

Reality TV isn't perfect, but it does one important thing – it introduces us to people we might never meet in person. In 1971, lilac-coiffed eccentric Quentin Crisp arrived into the homes of millions of unsuspecting viewers through fly-on-the-wall documentary *World in Action*. Half a century later, we're still talking about him – and there's been a host of iconic reality TV moments since:

The Real World

In the 1990s, Pedro Zamora, a gay, HIV-positive man, became a star on this MTV show, sensitively educating a generation of teenagers about the disease.

Eurovision

In 1998, Dana International, a Jewish-Israeli trans woman, won The Eurovision Song Contest with the female empowerment anthem 'Diva'.

Big Brother UK

Trans contestant Nadia Almada won in 2004, the second-highest-rated season ever.

Dancing With the Stars, America's Next Top Model

With his wins on both shows, Nyle DiMarco became one of the world's most visible deaf LGBTQ+ celebrities.

I'm a Celebrity

In season 15, Lady Colin Campbell became one of the first celebrities to reveal she was born intersex.

Today, HBO Max's *Legendary* and *We're Here*, Shudder's *Dragula* and the global *Drag Race* franchise continue to showcase and celebrate contestants of various gender identities, and consistently provide a platform for queer people of colour.

The Great British Gay Off

Queer representation on queer shows is great, but when it happens on cosy family competitions like *Bake Off*, it swells our hearts. Knowing that grannies are rooting for Tamal Ray, Cheun-Yan Tsou, Janusz Domagala and Sandro Farmhouse makes the show extra special. The rolling roster of funny lesbian and gay presenters like Sue Perkins, Sandi Toksvig and Matt Lucas makes it an even safer safe space.

Camp Reality TV Moments You Need to YouTube

Tyra Banks on America's Next Top Model cycle 4 (2005)

"I was rooting for you. We were all rooting for you. HOW DARE YOU!"

When Tiffany Richardson didn't seem as invested as *Top Model* host Tyra had hoped, Tyra eliminated her. When Tiffany tried to explain, Tyra went full-throttle medieval, delivering the hardest backhanded slap ever.

Cheryl Cole and Treyc Cohen on The X Factor season 7 (2010) via Harry Hill's TV Burp

"OK. Whenever you're ready."

"I'm ready."

"You said that with some determination."

"Whenever you're ready."

"I'm ready."

"OK."

"I'm ready."

"Whenever you're ready."

"I'm ready."

Cheryl and Treyc's repetitive back and forth in front of a bemused will.i.am at 'Judges Houses' is so ingrained in UK culture that over ten years later when Kitty Scott Claus and River Medway quoted it in DRUK3, we collectively clapped like seals.

The Real Housewives of New York season 6 (2014)

"The only thing that is artificial or fake about me is THIS."

How do you win an argument in the most shocking way? If you're Aviva Drescher, you throw your prosthetic leg across the restaurant – that'll shut everyone up.

Celebrity Big Brother season 17 (2016)

"David's Dead?"

When Angie Bowie's ex-husband David died, she told Tiffany Pollard in strict confidence, but in her grief failed to specify which David. Understandably, Tiffany thought she was referring to their housemate David: David Guest. A pitch-black comedy moment that may never be topped.

David Bowie is a role model for every letter in the LGBTQ+ family.

David Bowie is everything. A queer beacon who almost transcended humanity to become a divine alien. His music is as timeless as his visuals are legendary. He exploded gender-norms, wearing dresses, a full face of slap, and dying his hair flaming red. He filmed videos in drag, sang about the romances he had over his life, with boyfriends, groupies, his wife, trans girlfriend Romy Haag – and that was just an average Wednesday. He also did the thing that few people did in the 1970s and came out, publicly saying: "I'm gay" and "I'm bisexual" in interviews.

Bowie spoke directly to young people through his songs in a way people rarely did at the time: "Oh you pretty things, don't you know you're driving your mamas and papas insane?" No wonder girls, boys and everyone in between fell in love with him. And because he kept ch-ch-ch-changing, fans had the chance to fall in love with him over and over again, as they discovered each new persona: Ziggy Stardust, The Thin White Duke, Major Tom. His influence is so far-reaching that he's even been called the godfather of K-Pop.

Bowie's five queerest songs

1. Queen Bitch – Getting jealous when his boyfriend runs off with a trashy drag queen.
2. Boys Keep Swinging – Patriarchy commentary and bisexual sing-song. The music video is drag heaven – with Bowie sashaying the runway in three unforgettable looks.
3. John, I'm Only Dancing – Bi-poly plea.
4. Rebel Rebel – One of Bowie's most hard-rocking and iconic songs is a gender-fluid anthem beamed from 1974.
5. Jean Genie – Ode to singer Iggy Pop and clever wordplay on queer French writer Jean Genet.

Three Gen-Z Bowie covers

1. Space Oddity – Olivia Rodrigo
2. Changes – Zendaya, Willow Smith and Kiernan Shipka
3. Let's Dance – Miley Cyrus and David Byrne

A-Z of Queer Writers

There's been some page-turningly brilliant LGBTQ+ storytelling over the centuries. Here are some of the most inspirational figures.

Audre Lorde

A self-proclaimed 'Black, lesbian, warrior, mother poet' and key figure in the civil rights movement.

Brett Easton Ellis

Writer of the most exciting bisexual thrill-rides ever.

Charlie Jane Anders

Trans author Anders combines fantasy and dystopian sci-fi with a splash of magic in *All the Birds in the Sky* (2016).

Denton Welch

A brilliant outsider who could teach Wednesday Adams a thing or two about being an awkward teenager.

E. M. Forster

His gay novel *Maurice* (1971) was so controversial that it wasn't published until his death. It's actually adorbs.

Federico García Lorca

A playwright and poet who was responsible for bringing new life to Spanish theatre. In 1936, he was shot, likely for being a liberal and homosexual.

Gertrude Stein

A patron of the arts and author of *Q.E.D.* (1903), one of the first coming-out stories.

Henry James

James wrote classic ghost story *The Turn of the Screw* (1898). Also, almost certainly a massive closet-case.

Ifti Nasim

The first out gay Pakistani poet described his experience as a gay Muslim in many works in Urdu, Punjabi and English.

Jeanette Winterson

Her debut novel *Oranges Are Not the Only Fruit* (1985) was THEE lesbian coming-of-age novel of the 1980s.

Kacen Callender

This award-winning Black queer trans author's novel *Felix Ever After* (2020) tackles the intersections of trans identity, sexuality and race, inspired by their own lived experience.

Leslie Fienberg

Fienberg's exploration of masculinity as a self-described 'anti-racist, white, working-class, secular, Jewish, transgender, lesbian female' is canon. Read *Stone Butch Blues* (1993).

Mary Renault

Lesbian author Renault's novel *The Charioteer* (1953) is one of the first and best to explore post-WWII same-sex love. Secret tip: the audiobook is dreamy heaven.

Naoise Dolan

Her debut novel *Exciting Times* (2020) was the bisexual dissection of modern life we didn't know we needed.

Ocean Vuong

The highly acclaimed *On Earth We're Briefly Gorgeous* (2019) whisks us through heart-poundingly poetic moments.

Poppy Z. Brite

PZB is the pen name of trans man Billy Martin, who found fame in the 1990s writing queer-leaning Gothic horror.

Quentin Crisp

The Naked Civil Servant (1968) is one of the first relatable books on finding yourself as a queer person at a time – the 1930s – when it was not only dangerous but illegal.

Rivers Solomon

A non-binary, intersex author who uses they/them/fae/faer pronouns. Obsessed with this. Take flight with their debut novel, *An Unkindness of Ghosts* (2017).

Sarah Waters

Historical romance can be extremely sexually normative – but Waters has *women* ripping bodices for a change.

Torrey Peters

The author of *Detransition Baby* (2021), a runaway success that explored trans lives in the most page-turny, feely way.

Ursula K. Le Guin

Though she was not LGBTQ+ , Le Guin explored identity in her 'genderless' novel *The Left Hand of Darkness* (1969).

Virginia Woolf

Orlando (1928) would be shocking enough if it was written by an averagely talented writer. Lucky for us, Woolf is one of the greatest ever writers in English. Slam dunk.

Walt Whitman

The daddy of US poetry, who wrote some of the most homoerotic verse ever in *Leaves of Grass*, way back in 1860, turning farmhands and soldiers into sensual heroes.

Xavier Villaurrutia

Latin America's first famous out gay writer. He also founded Mexico's first experimental theatre group in 1928.

Yukio Mishima

Japanese writer Mishima's *Confessions of a Mask* (1949) is a radical novel about a boy wrestling with gay feelings, and brought this complicated writer worldwide fame.

Zora Neale Hurston

Netizens fully argue about Hurston's sexuality, and I'm sure she'd be flattered that so many people still care. But the leading light of the Harlem Renaissance left enough bisexual breadcrumbs to give us pause for thought.

Musical Theatre Starter Pack

Once upon a time, show queens were the centre of queer culture . . . and, boy, did they make a song and dance about it.

If you've watched the jazz-hands joy-fest that is *Schmigadoon!* on Apple TV, you might have noticed that it's built on 10,001 musical theatre references per second. Only a Jedi master of musicals will know every reference being made by this gayest of shows, but there are some queer faves every musicals newbie should check out.

THE DANCEY ONES

A Chorus Line – One singular sensational day of dance auditions.

Hairspray – Corny showcase for big girls, racial inclusion, drag queens and roach-stomping.

West Side Story – A tender Romeo and Juliet love story in the world of gang warfare.

THE HISTORICAL ONES

Six – Divorced, beheaded, died, divorced, beheaded and had an utterly wicked time.

Hamilton – Lin-Manuel Miranda's hip-hop history lesson schools all the modern musicals.

Les Misérables – Revolutionary French misery.

THE ONES WITH BITE

Wicked – The Witches of Oz defy expectations – and gravity.

Cabaret – Life is one . . . until the Nazis seize power.

Chicago – Velma and Roxie go directly to jail and do not pass an opportunity to wiggle their limbs.

THE GENDER-EXPLORING ONES

Everyone's Talking About Jamie – School's a right drag – well, it can be, if you're lucky.

Rent – Operatic tragedy with baked-in diversity and LGBTQ+ activism.

Kinky Boots – The shoe must go on for this feisty drag entrepreneur.

Fascinating Queers: Alvin Ailey

If you think dance seems like a stuck-up art form that you don't 'get', chances are you've not heard of Alvin Ailey's incredible, inclusive dance company.

Ailey was a pioneering Black, queer, working-class, neurodivergent dancer and choreographer in 1950s America, a time when it was illegal to be gay in most states and racial segregation was still federal law. Ailey formed his dance group, The Alvin Ailey American Dance Theater, in 1958, giving opportunities and a voice to his company of mostly Black dancers, and providing a safe space for young queer people of colour to express themselves without fear of discrimination. He continued his career in the 1960s, 70s and 80s, revolutionising 20th-century modern dance by incorporating Black culture and challenging ideas about what 'high art' was. He died in 1989, but his company is still going strong, and his legacy continues to inspire contemporary dance companies who are looking to incorporate social themes in their work. His most celebrated work, *Revelations*, is so popular that it was used in the 1968 opening ceremony of the Olympic Games.

'Lewd and criminal tendencies'

Like many artists of his time, Ailey was private about his queerness – and it's no wonder. When his company went on tour in 1962, the FBI added him to their list of people to watch and referred to his sexuality as 'lewd and criminal tendencies'. So, while Ailey celebrated Black culture in his work, his sexuality was left largely unexplored.

Two more dance troupes to catch

Les Ballets Trockadero de Monte Carlo

In this all-male ballet company, the guys actually get to dance the good parts (i.e. the girls' parts), be-wigged and en-pointe in tutus. The company has been going for years (nearly 50) and it's incredible. Their shows are very funny, but the dancing is no joke – all members are professionals.

Sean Dorsey Dance

Sean Dorsey is America's foremost trans choreographer and artistic director, creating dance pieces that lift up and explore trans and gender-non-conforming narratives. His company has been operating for nearly two decades. At a time when the identity discourse can be overwhelming, immersing yourself in something real, intimate and physical can offer an insightful alternative to plain back-and-forth talk.

Essential Gay Films

A selection of essential queer movies to add to your watch list – and a few of the lessons we can learn from them.

Beautiful Thing (15), dir. Hettie MacDonald, 1996

Queer love on a council estate may be a beautiful thing, but it's not easy; Mama Cass helps.

Bend It Like Beckham (12), dir. Gurinder Chadha, 2002

Just because two girls don't kiss doesn't mean they're not rampantly gay for each other.

Blue Jean (15), dir. Georgia Oakley, 2022

Separating your 'authentic queer life' from your regular day-to-day life is a moral conundrum.

Booksmart (15), dir. Olivia Wilde, 2019

Being good is fine, but having fun is important too, so don't forget to let loose and break the rules sometimes.

Bottoms (15), dir. Emma Seligman, 2023

Lesbians aren't losers, they are hard-hitting and hilarious as [bleep].

Brokeback Mountain (15), dir. Ang Lee, 2005

The closet is a dark and destructive place. It's better to have loved and lost than to never have loved at all.

But I'm a Cheerleader (15), dir. Jamie Babbit, 1999

You cannot 'convert' someone's sexuality, you just turn them into really good liars. The people who make the rules are generally the first to break them.

Carol (15), dir. Todd Haynes, 2012

The most wonderful time of the year is when a classy blonde divorcée whisks you off your aching feet.

God's Own Country (15), dir. Francis Lee, 2017

Gay people exist outside of cities and so does rampant xenophobia. People aren't really bothered what you get up to in the bedroom, or barn.

Les Chansons D'Amour (15) dir. Christophe Honoré, 2007

Bisexual love is real, you just might have to stick around for a while to see it.

Maurice (15), dir. James Ivory, 1987

You will survive first love. You can be gay and have a happy ending. Real is better than rich.

Moonlight (15), dir. Barry Jenkins, 2016

We all need love and emotional support. Sometimes you have to wait ages for romance – hang in there. Also, be brave because people are awful, but you don't have to be.

Parting Glances (15), dir. Bill Sherwood, 1986

Gays aren't just pretty boy stereotypes. Falling in love with the wrong people sucks. Tell the person you love that you love them before it's too late.

Pride (15), dir. Matthew Warchus, 2014

Not everyone hates us. In fact with very little persuasion, we can uncover allies in surprising places. Give people a chance.

Rocky Horror Picture Show (12), dir. Jim Sherman, 1975

Don't dream it. Be it. Making the perfect man has its drawbacks. Stockings and suspenders suit everyone.

Tangerine (15), dir. Sean Baker, 2015

When the daily grind gets you down and the situation turns wild, you're going to want a best friend and an armour-plated sense of humour. Actual trans actors playing trans roles.

Tár (15), dir. Todd Field, 2022

Women can do anything that men can, and that includes being a total utter nightmare monster that we hate-fancy.

The Adventures of Priscilla, Queen of the Desert (15), dir. Stephan Elliot, 1994

Self-expression can cause grief and ridicule while at the same time offering a lifeline.

The Boys in the Band (15), dir. William Friedkin, 1970

Parties thrown by gays are a laugh-riot, until liquor and

self-loathing intervene, then dancing turns into drunk-dialling and crying.

The Kids Are All Right (15), dir. Lisa Cholodenko, 2010

Families come in different shapes and sizes and all of them struggle to make things run smoothly. Lesbian and bisexual women make really cute mums, but they're not perfect.

Tomboy (U), dir. Céline Sciamma, 2011

Children love to play dress up; sometimes it's more than that, sometimes it's not.

Victim (12), dir. Basil Dearden, 1961

Queer people are always watching their backs to see who is coming for them, but actually everyone is a victim of something. Homophobes don't ask to be brought up by bigots. Hate is learned.

XXY (15), dir. Lucía Puenzo, 2007

The most celebrated film that explores the intersex experience is an Argentinian movie from 2007. *XXY* is about 15-year-old Alex and their struggle to negotiate puberty and explore their gender beyond the restrictive and not-altogether-true 'assigned female' identity. It won the Critics Grand Prize at the Cannes Film Festival.

Subtext or Straightwashed?

Hollywood has a habit of erasing or diminishing us, which accidentally turned us into gay detectives.

Straightwashing – when a character who is widely believed to be queer is presented in a way that minimises their true identity. It's lying by omission.

Queer coding/subtext – when queerness is implied, but we're left to guess if the character is actually queer or not. Queer coded characters are those who seem real gay, but no one actually says it. Perfect for villains like Pokémon's Team Rocket or Mrs Danvers in *Rebecca*.

Subtext is great for telling us something bubbling beneath the surface of a story. As a rule, that shouldn't be the sexual orientation of the characters. We exist, dammit. Show us US. Here are a few films guilty of hinting at queerness but never quite owning up to it:

Red River (U), dir. Howard Hawks and Arthur Rosson, 1948

The gun swap scene from this film is the flirtiest thing ever – gay actor Montgomery Clift delivers a masterclass in subtlety and subtext previously unseen on the big screen. "That's a good-looking gun . . . can I see it?" Pause. "Maybe you'd like to see mine?" Gulp.

Rebel Without a Cause (PG), dir. Nicholas Ray, 1955

Plato, played by a 16-year-old Sal Mineo, is gay. End of. He has a picture of Alan Ladd in his locker. "Not ready to come out yet?" asks James Dean. "Promise you nothing will happen if you do." Most audiences focus on the love story between Dean and Natalie Wood, but gay men could see that Mineo was just as in love with Jimmy as Natalie was.

Star Wars: The Force Awakens (12), dir. J. J. Abrams, 2015

Finn and Poe in the *Star Wars* franchise aren't queer, but they could be, just like Elsa in the *Frozen* franchise or Cap and Bucky in *Captain America* could be. The fact movie studios almost never lean into fanfic and shipping just seems mean at this point. A Finn-Poe romance could've been a huge win for the gays – but no, instead we got James Corden in *The Prom*. #thankful #blessed #joke

Oceans 8 (12), dir. Gary Ross, 2018

We're not told that Cate Blanchett and Sandra Bullock are a couple in the movie, but of course they are. Just look at them. They feed each other, for crying out loud!

Black Panther (12), dir. Ryan Coogler, 2018

The screenwriter admitted that a gay relationship between female bodyguards Okoye and Ayo had been on the cards, but it never materialised. The follow-up film, *Wakanda Forever* (2022), fed us an extra crumb: a kiss on the forehead. So generous. You shouldn't have.

UK Drag

In many ways, drag, a favourite art form in the UK, was the first special effect, instantly confusing and transporting us. It's been doing that for hundreds and hundreds of years. Here are a few highlights of the UK's rich and varied drag history . . .

Princess Seraphina

In 1732, a man who often went about in female attire was brought before a court of law. Princess Seraphina (as she was known to everyone) was not the one in trouble; someone had stolen her clothes. Brutes. Seraphina is considered the first drag queen in the UK, but we might also think of her as an early trans pioneer.

Principal boy is a girl – shock!

Since 1819, when Eliza Povey first played the role of Jack in *Jack and the Beanstalk*, the 'principal boy' role in pantomimes has regularly been played by a woman. Over the decades, Peter Pan, Prince Charming and Dick Whittington have all regularly been played by women. When Cilla Black took to the stage as Aladdin in 1971, she was credited with reviving the trend.

Cinderella's Sapphic reading

While Prince Charming is often played by a woman, so too is his dashing best friend, Dandini – along with Cinderella herself, of course. The male actors, meanwhile, are relegated to the roles of ugly sisters, turning a simple, regressive fairy tale into something far more subversive.

Vesta Tilley

Celebrated male-impersonator Vesta Tilley made up to £1,000 in a week in the early 1900s – worth about £116,000 in today's money – and is thought to be the highest-earning British woman of her era. Tilley wore men's clothes (including underwear) and sang romantic songs such as 'I'm the Idol of the Girls'. She retired in 1919 after a career spanning over 50 years, donating the proceeds of her farewell tour to various children's hospitals around the country. We tip our hat to you, Vesta.

Lily Savage

Paul O'Grady's iconic creation Lily Savage could be the UK's most successful drag queen of our lifetimes. She was brassy, surly and silly-funny, and in the 90s and 00s had us in a televisual headlock.

Schoolboy drag

In the 1980s, two of the biggest children's entertainers on TV were husband and wife team The Krankies, who pretended to be a dad and his naughty little boy. Sound strange? It was.

Danny La Rue

When we think of 'old-school UK drag', if we're old enough, we think of Danny La Rue in an opulent gown, dripping ostrich feathers and diamonds, and a towering blonde wig. The look is very beautiful and theatrical but quickly became seen as old-fashioned. This didn't stop Danny La Rue being one of the UK's most famous entertainers in the 60s and 70s.

Alternative Miss World

The wildest gender-scrambled event in the world is the semi-occasional Alternative Miss World pageant. Founded in 1972 by sculptor Andrew Logan, and inspired by Crufts – yes, you read that right – it's still going strong. Past participants include Divine, Leigh Bowery, Zandra Rhodes, Ruby Wax and Tim Curry. Derek Jarman won in 1975 as Miss Crepe Suzette and, in 1986, Grayson Perry entered as Jesus. And it's not just celebrities who take part – anyone can enter. Watch the 2011 documentary about the spectacle: *The British Guide to Showing Off.*

The WORLD'S most popular drag queen?

We know we shouldn't compare drag queens, but to give you some idea of how popular Brazilian drag superstar **Pabllo Vittar** is, take a look at her IG stats and let the numbers sink in. She is the most followed drag queen in the world by a whopping amount. She's collaborated with Lady Gaga and Charli XCX, performed at Coachella, and, as of writing, has three million monthly listeners on Spotify alone. She was the first drag queen to be nominated for a Grammy and the first to win an MTV Award for best Brazilian artist. In 2022, she hosted Brazil's drag queen reality show for HBO Max, *Queen Stars*. In 2023, she headlined Manchester Pride.

As they say in Portuguese: *glamorosa, fabulosa, espetacular*.

An LGBTQ+ Library for Every Mood

If you're craving some good reading, but don't know where to start, give these pages a flick.

When you want to laugh your retro socks off
Tales of the City by Armistead Maupin

When all you fancy is an ace journey of self-discovery
Loveless by Alice Oseman

When you want an apocalyptic bisexual adventure
Grasshopper Jungle by Andrew A. Smith

When you're thirsting for an ungodly ancient epic
Song of Achilles by Madeline Miller

When you're in the mood for a lesbian Cinderella story
Ash by Malindo Lo

When you need a trans-boy-ghost-boy coming-of-age story
Cemetery Boy by Aiden Thomas

When you crave a cracking mystery to keep you up at night
Report For Murder – Val McDermid

When you need Asian representation and rock'n'roll
The Buddha of Suburbia by Hanif Kureshi

When you're after multicultural lesbian YA
The Henna Wars by Adiba Jaigirdar

When you hunger to devour some gothic gayness
The Vampire Lestat by Anne Rice

When you need a sprawling family saga with an intersex protagonist
Middlesex – Jeffrey Eugenides

When you need a powerful verse novel about finding yourself through drag
The Black Flamingo – Dean Atta

When you're ready to be really, really angry
The Miseducation of Cameron Post by Emily M. Danforth

When you want to escape into a cute queer romance
Love and Other Disasters by Anita Kelly

When you want a straightforward (but not too straight) high school story
Simon vs. the Homo Sapiens Agenda by Becky Albertalli

When you want a royal page-turner that's fire emoji
Red, White and Royal Blue – Casey McQuiston

As Seen Onscreen: The Big Questions

A lot of issues seem to crop up over and over in online comments sections. Let's get to the bottom of them.

Is queerbaiting* real?

No, not in real life. Everyone should be allowed to be as performatively queer as they want, and have room to dabble and discover. The more transgressive the better. When it comes to fictional representation, however, queerbaiting is very real. If a director or screenwriter says that a character is gay but fails to round them out with exciting queer narratives, then what's the point? By the same token, thirst-trapping viewers with flirty scenes but not delivering the goods is childish and sly. Grow up. Make the sexually adventurous James Bond bi and sod the homophobic fanboys!

*Flirting with queerness but showing none of the receipts.

Is Hollywood homophobic?

Hollywood is homophobic by default, because it upholds the views (and prejudices) of society. It does so to make money – and Hollywood is a business; all it cares about is money. If guys kissing made money at the box office, then every Avengers movie would be about men of iron falling in love with other men of varying alloys. Hundreds of thousands of movies have been made over a hundred years and how often are queer people the hero in a mainstream movie? Patiently waiting.

Should queer characters always be played by queer actors?

No, ideally, the best person should get the job – BUT that means gay and lesbian, bisexual and non-binary actors should get an equal chance to play ALL roles. In recent years, openly gay actors have finally been cast in romantic, leading straight roles. The swoon-potential of **Jonathan Bailey** in *Bridgerton* and **Andrew Scott** in *Fleabag* was never in question. We should also stop being so square as to assume that heterosexual-seeming people haven't had homosexual encounters or feelings, or require them to take a metaphorical lie-detector test to prove that they're one of us, as **Kit Connor** and **Jameela Jamil** felt forced to. Wanting equality is a good a thing, but policing who can explore sexuality and gender expression is its own form of bigotry. However, when it comes to trans roles, I think we can all agree that trans actors should play them. Watching cis men and women play trans roles used to be the norm, but then so was blackface and yellowface. Thankfully, times move on. Humiliating a section of society by pretending to be them is an acting challenge we can do away with – just hire trans actors. Watch the excellent documentary *Disclosure* for the full story.

What do we need more of in terms of representation?

The one place queer characters would fit brilliantly, but are rarely seen, is genre movies such as horror, sci-fi, fantasy, mystery and westerns. Here, the sexual or romantic orientation of the lead doesn't matter for the story, but we are more than who we sleep with. It would be nice to see movies like this with a queer lead.

When it comes to movies and TV, the representation of queer characters often gives us a lot to live up to in the real world. Lesbians are fantastically strong and powerful women while every gay man has a good sense of humour. We basically see the version of queer that straight people like, which usually involves us giving something to them: protection or LOLs. I know it sounds backwards, but we need more underachieving, chaotic role models, please:

- A flaky lesbian
- A gay man with zero bants
- A trans woman who shops at Next

Is shipping bad?

Some people think shipping two celebrities is bullying. It's not, it's fun – until it's not, right? Imagining a world where Edward and Jacob from *Twilight* are in love is cute and sexy and not that deep. It's a way of extending our love beyond watching the films or reading the books. When it comes to real people, content is clicks, and that's great for the brand, unless they're utterly battered by it. It's hard to say if a star like Taylor Swift is upset by her ships, or Harry Styles for that matter, but years-long campaigns of conspiracies must feel like a version of harassment. At this point we can say it would be healthier to get a life.

The Bechdel test

The Bechdel test was thought up by lesbian comic book writer and artist **Alison Bechdel** to point out that women in movies are often two-dimensional cut-outs, woefully lacking in meaningful characterisation. To pass the test, a film must have two named female characters talking to each other about something other than a man. There's a TikTok captioned 'Lord of the Rings Trilogy, but it's EVERY scene where two female characters interact'. In over ten hours of film, only two words are uttered by one female to another: "Where's Mama?" Nowadays most movies do better, with the likes of *Don't Worry Darling, Tár, Scream, Babylon* and *Glass Onion* all passing. Films featuring the male protagonist in the title regularly fail: *Elvis, Lightyear, Morbius, Pinocchio, The Northman.*

How Queer Are You?

It's not a contest, but if it was, would you win?

Whenever someone homophobically stereotypes a queer person as Kylie-loving or cat-owning it can hurt (sometimes because it's true). But it doesn't *really* hurt because cats and Kylie are awesome and we love what we love with zero shame. Straight culture invented 'guilty pleasures' – we don't know her. How many other fantastic ways are you stereotypically queer as a pink-haired goose? Take the quiz.

Part 1

Which of the following obsess you more than the average human?

Disney
Doctor Who
Veganism
Hyperpop
The Sims
Body hair
Barbie
Women's soccer
Broadway musicals
Second-wave feminism
Cottagecore
Eurovision
Cats
Taylor Swift
WitchTok
Kylie
Fashion
Horror films
Star Trek
The Victorian period

Your score
/20

Part 2

Guys and NBs, which of these do you own?

Plaid shirt
Blue jeans (well-worn and snug)
Jogging bottoms/sweatpants
Nice blouse
High-waisted trousers
Crop top
Dungarees
Khaki nylon flight jacket
Vest (undershirt/tank top)
See-through top
Short shorts
Harness
Neckerchief
Pearl necklace
Speedos

Your score
/15

Girls and NBs, which of these do you own?

Plaid shirt
Skinny black jeans
Button-down shirt
Denim shirt
Blazer
Boxer shorts/boxer briefs
Socially conscious slogan tee
Beanie
Boots (DMs, combat, hiking, Converse)
Birkenstocks
Vest (undershirt/tank top)
Leather bracelet
Dickie bow and/or braces
Overalls/boiler suit/dungarees
Chunky specs

Your score
/15

Part 3

How many of these apply?

- You drink iced coffee
- You have a nose piercing
- You have an undercut
- You've dyed your hair turquoise/pink/purple
- You have a stan account on social media
- You like to cuff your trousers
- You have/had a 'difficult' relationship with your dad
- You're always late
- You have a minor crush on the foxes in *Zootopia* and *Robin Hood*
- You've been in a school play
- You've argued that Gaga/Lana/Kate Bush is the best
- You've snogged half of your friends
- You walk really fast
- You wear make-up – but only eyeliner and mascara
- You have a favourite lip balm
- You can't sit properly on a chair
- You own more than one thing with a rainbow on it
- You like stationery – like, *really* like stationery
- You believe in astrology, especially Virgos and Aquarians
- You know what 'zshoozh' means

Your score
/20

Add your scores together

Less than 15
Call yourself queer? Get out!

Between 16 and 30
Wow, you're an uncannily balanced human – how do you do it? You don't let your sexuality and gender identity rule your life – weird.

More than 31
You're a massive queer triumph. Science should study you. Go and submit yourself to the nearest university for immediate investigation and preservation.

Note: Please don't take this too seriously. Of course, some queer people prefer dogs, wouldn't be seen dead in a crop top and detest all Australian pop stars.

Gothic Horror: We Invented That

Gothic horror is essentially stories set in creepy old houses where the sense of dread lingers like a sly servant. There may be fractious ghosts. Windows will bang. Hinges will not have seen a drop of WD40. Brilliant fun – and, somehow, very queer.

Creepy Castle 101

Horace Walpole's book *The Castle of Otranto* (1764) is considered the first ever gothic novel, inspiring centuries of variations on his themes of supernatural goings-on: creepy old buildings, doors closing by themselves, secret passages, hidden identities and ancient prophecies. You can go and visit Horace's flamboyant old pad in Twickenham, west London, if you fancy a creepy wander.

Frankenstein's bisexual mother

Looking for the most badass woman in English literature? Try **Mary Shelley**, who wrote *Frankenstein*, one of the earliest gothic horror novels, in 1818, when she was only 20. After Mary's husband, romantic poet Percy Shelley, perished in a boating accident, Mary carried his literal calcified heart with her, everywhere she went. Goth queen, we worship. It gets extra spicy when she admitted in a letter to getting 'tousy-mousy for women' – which most scholars agree means being attracted to them. Add it to your lexicon.

Something to sink your teeth into . . .

Vampire novels were some of the earliest gothic books with queer themes. In 1872, **Sheridan Le Fanu's** novella *Carmilla* was released, starring a character who forms a close and Sapphic relationship with a vampire. Bram Stoker took inspiration from Le Fanu with his famous novel *Dracula*. Stoker fascinates queer scholars, specifically because of a gushing love letter he wrote to celebrated American gay poet Walt Whitman, after reading *Leaves of Grass*. Stoker wrote that he "felt his heart leap [. . .] across the Atlantic".

Edward Gorey – the original Tim Burton

It's safe to say that Neil Gaiman, Guillermo del Toro and Tim Burton owe a debt to the macabre picture books of Edward Gorey. His elegantly scratchy drawings conjure a Victorian world filled with the disturbed and the absurd. The eccentric 'grandaddy of Goth' was reluctant to label his sexuality. In an 1980 interview, he said, "I've never said I was gay, and I've never said I wasn't. A lot of people would say that I wasn't because I never do anything about it." Whether gay, asexual, emo and over it, Gorey's work is ghoulishly good.

Three essential gothic novels

- *Strange Case of Doctor Jekyll and Mr Hyde* by **Robert Louis Stevenson**. A man fighting his 'monstrous' urges. Hmm, what might that be a metaphor for?
- *The Picture of Dorian Gray* by **Oscar Wilde**. A tale of hedonism and sin by one of our most famous gay authors.
- *Rebecca* by **Daphne du Maurier**. A tale of obsession with a foreboding lesbian love – go on then.

The Queerest Art Tour

Queer art, we love to see it. Now *you* can with this handy guide to the coolest artworks in the UK.

Aberdeen Art Gallery and Museums

- Rosa Bonheur – *Changing Pastures*, 1863
- Dorothy Johnstone – *Black and Yellow*, 1920

Aldeburgh beach, Suffolk

- Maggi Hambling – *Scallop: A Conversation with the Sea*, 2003

Dundee Art Galleries

- Francis Cadell – *The White Shirt*, 1922

Edinburgh College of Art

- Eduardo Paolozzi – *Josephine Baker*, 1997

Jersey Heritage Trust

- Claude Cahun – *I'm in Training, Don't Kiss Me*, 1927

Leeds Art Gallery

- Gwen John – *Chloë Boughton-Leigh*, 1910–1914
- Francis Bacon – *Painting*, 1950

Manchester Art Gallery

- Auguste Charles Mengin – *Sappho*, 1877

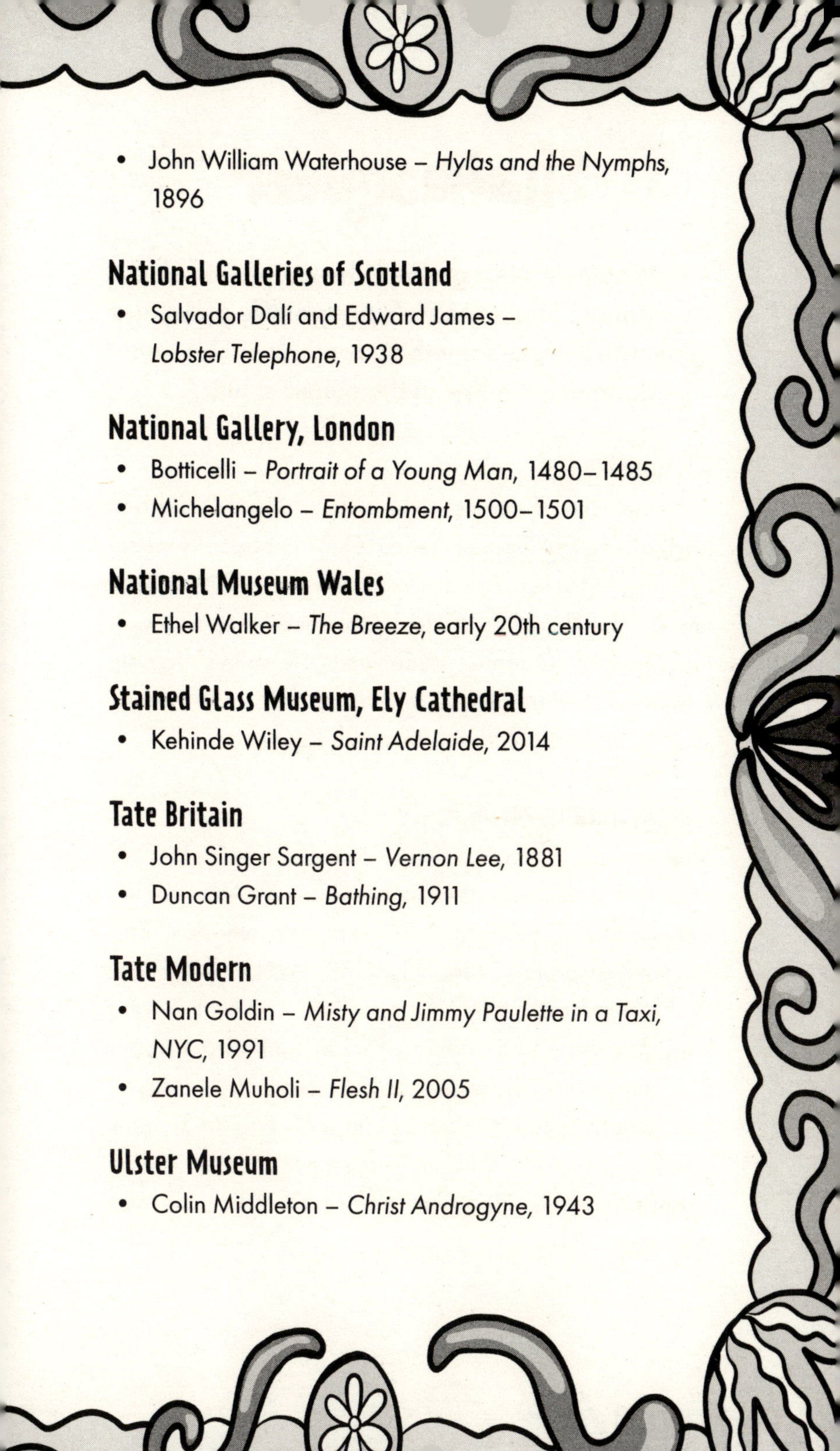

- John William Waterhouse – *Hylas and the Nymphs*, 1896

National Galleries of Scotland

- Salvador Dalí and Edward James – *Lobster Telephone*, 1938

National Gallery, London

- Botticelli – *Portrait of a Young Man*, 1480–1485
- Michelangelo – *Entombment*, 1500–1501

National Museum Wales

- Ethel Walker – *The Breeze*, early 20th century

Stained Glass Museum, Ely Cathedral

- Kehinde Wiley – *Saint Adelaide*, 2014

Tate Britain

- John Singer Sargent – *Vernon Lee*, 1881
- Duncan Grant – *Bathing*, 1911

Tate Modern

- Nan Goldin – *Misty and Jimmy Paulette in a Taxi, NYC*, 1991
- Zanele Muholi – *Flesh II*, 2005

Ulster Museum

- Colin Middleton – *Christ Androgyne*, 1943

Shakesqueer

Whatever your gender identity or sexual orientation, Shakespeare's progressive plays and poems will have something for you. Buckle your doublet for a few of the queerest bits . . .

As You Like It

Rosalind, one of the main characters, dresses as a boy and calls herself Ganymede: a name that basically meant 'gay boy' (gay was not a term that existed in Elizabethan times). She then has a de facto queer romance with leading man Orlando. Meanwhile, Rosalind's cousin Celia tells her that she will "love no man in good earnest", suggesting her real love is reserved for women.

The Mysterious Mr W.H.

Shakespeare wrote 154 love sonnets, and dedicated them not to his wife, but to a certain Mr W.H. Some believe this to be his patron Henry Wriothesley, Earl of Southampton. Others think it's William Herbert, Earl of Pembroke. Mr W.H.'s identity is so elusive and intriguing that Oscar Wilde wrote an entire story about it. Shakespeare addressed 126 sonnets to an unnamed man simply called the 'fair youth', including the famous 'Shall I compare thee to a summer's day?'. Some experts think this 'fair youth' and Mr W.H. are one and the same.

Twelfth Night

The star of the play, Viola, is a gender-fluid cause of mischief and mayhem, who dresses up as a young man called Cesario. Both Duke Orsino and noblewoman Olivia fall head over heels for her. Shakespeare basically explains that gender isn't important when it comes to who we love – whether Viola is a boy called Cesario, a girl going by her given name, or both at the same time, is irrelevant. It's the person – who has both masculine and feminine charms – that Orsino and Olivia fall for.

Did Shakespeare invent drag?

The word 'drag' is generally assumed to have come from the theatre. The term may have come about to describe male actors playing women's roles in Shakespearean plays, 'dragging' their dresses across the stage. The other suggestion is that the word is an acronym: D.R.A.G. (Dressed Resembling A Girl), something all Shakespeare's male actors did when they played the heroines.

Unforgettable Queer Movie Moments

Every one of these moments in cinema history still holds a remarkable power . . .

Wings (PG), dir. William A. Wellman, 1927

The first same-sex kiss in Hollywood history – the most tenderly shot, romantically scored embrace of two handsome young men you'll ever see.

Morocco (PG), dir. Josef von Sternberg, 1930

Marlene Dietrich glides onto the screen in a tuxedo and top hat, plucks a flower from behind a woman's ear and kisses her on the mouth: the first lead actress in a movie to kiss another woman. No one is safe from her charms.

Bringing Up Baby (U), dir. Howard Hawks, 1938

Cary Grant explaining why he's wearing a woman's dressing gown: "Because I just went gay all of a sudden." This was especially daring, because, according to numerous sources, the matinée idol was at the very least bi.

Some Like It Hot (PG), dir. Billy Wilder, 1959

Winner of the prize for best last line. When Jack Lemmon drags up as a woman to escape the mafia, he inadvertently gets a boyfriend. When Jack tells him, "I'm a man," his lover replies, "Nobody's perfect!"

If . . . (15), dir. Lindsay Anderson, 1968

Bobby Warwick and Rupert Webster's aching depiction of teenage longing is worth watching – it's the first schoolboys-in-love story on film

Cabaret (15), dir. Bob Fosse, 1972

When Sally (Liza Minnelli) reveals she's cheating on boyfriend Brian with Max the German Baron, Brian admits that he is too and it's the first bisexual gotcha in cinema. *Willkommen* representation!

Looking For Langston (15), dir. Isaac Julien, 1989

A pair of handsome Black men dance in tuxedos. A high-gloss, Old Hollywood depiction of queer men of colour in another place and another time. An homage to Langston Hughes and the Harlem Renaissance (see page 66) that exists in its own sensual dreamworld free from racism and homophobia.

Mulholland Drive (15), dir. David Lynch, 2001

A mysterious dark-haired woman gets it on with a fresh-faced blonde – and it's fire. Film critics call this spiralling Hollywood mystery one of the greatest films of the 20th century. Can't agree more.

Everything Everywhere All at Once (15), dir. Daniel Kwan and Daniel Scheinert, 2022

In another universe, Jamie-Lee Curtis is having a romantic relationship with Michelle Yeoh, except with sausage fingers. Evolution is no fool. No one seemed to talk about the fact that EEAAO was super gay, but it is.

Trans Pioneers

Inspirational transgender artists are out there getting on with it. No biggie – except, it is.

FAY PRESTO

In the 80s and 90s, trans woman Fay Presto was one of TV's most famous magicians. Renowned to this day for her close-up, sleight-of-hand magic, she has a brilliant rapport with her audience, and began doing street-style illusions years before they took off in the mainstream. She regularly appeared on light entertainment shows, and do you know how much of an uproar there was? None. The fact she'd changed her sex was interesting, something to mention – like having a twin or piercing blue eyes – and then everyone just moved on. Would her tricks be good? Could we work out how she did it? What's for tea?

When Fay transitioned, she was booted out of the prestigious Magic Circle, which had a men-only policy. As the most successful female magician at that time, she began to campaign for women to be admitted to the group. Time waved its wand and, in 1991, women were finally allowed to join. Since then, Fay has become a gold-star member of the Inner Magic Circle and is still very much an active magician. She's so funny, relaxed and beautiful – go watch her clips on YouTube.

BILLY TIPTON

Billy Tipton was a jazz musician in the 1930s, 40s and 50s. He was a bandleader, pianist and saxophonist, who recorded a couple of records, but never made into the big time. His story would likely have been completely forgotten – but upon his death in 1989, he was discovered to have been assigned female at birth. Nobody knew.

Billy began binding his chest in the 1930s and lived his entire life as a man, managing this without surgery or hormones. He was described after his death as 'funny', 'personable' and 'gentle'. He adopted three children with his common-law wife and even became a scoutmaster.

TRACEY NORMAN

Tracey Norman was the world's first Black trans female model. Her success story is like a fairy tale where the lesson is 'believe in yourself and be as brave as you dare to be'. In the mid 1970s, Tracey was interested in getting into modelling and would slip into fashion shows to learn all she could. But she didn't hang around waiting for a big break. A split-second opportunity arose when she saw a group of Black models walking into a casting, and she took it, boldly following them in. It was here that Tracey bagged her first job, an *Italian Vogue* editorial worth $1,500. Boom.

Tracey went on to have a career that included modelling for Clairol hair dye. It wasn't plain sailing though. She kept her transgender identity hidden when she started out and was sacked from an Avon campaign when her assigned gender came to light. But Clairol came through in 2016, when they invited her to be the face of their latest campaign, at age 63.

LANA AND LILLY WACHOWSKI

Lana and Lilly Wachowski are without doubt two of the coolest and most successful creators, who happen to be trans, on the planet. You can totally read *The Matrix* movies as a trans allegory. The sisters made the films before transitioning, so the trans narrative isn't overt, however by the time the siblings made fan-fave Netflix series *Sense8*, the full, gloriously fluid queer spectrum was being explored.

JAMES FORD

James Ford was a contestant on Netflix's *Next in Fashion*, and was a big deal in 2023. Was it 'gotcha!' stunt-casting to have the dashing designer reveal that he was trans? Or was it simply reflecting a fact of life: some men are trans? Whatever your take, James was a delightful presence.

CHRISTINE JORGENSEN

When Christine Jorgensen had gender-affirming surgery in the 1950s, she became an instant celebrity. The story of a US army GI becoming a woman was too much for the press to handle and they splashed sensationalist headlines over their front pages. Jorgensen took the fame thrust upon her with grace and charm, providing a much-needed voice for those with gender dysphoria.

A-list LGBTQ+ Biopics

Learning queer history doesn't have to be a slog, so grab some popcorn and settle down for some infotainment with these big-screen life stories about icons from all corners of culture.

MUSICIANS

Elton John: 70s piano man, film score composer, Donald Duck impersonator. Played by Taron Egerton in *Rocket Man* (2019).

Joan Jett: The coolest woman in rock'n'roll. Played by Kristen Stewart in *The Runaways* (2010).

Ma Rainey: Jazz Age blues legend. Played by Viola Davis in *Ma Rainey's Black Bottom* (2020).

Freddie Mercury: The greatest front-man of all time. Played by Rami Malek in *Bohemian Rhapsody* (2018).

WRITERS

Allen Ginsberg: American Beat poet who found fame in the 50s and 60s. Played by Daniel Radcliffe in *Kill Your Darlings* (2013) and James Franco in *Howl* (2010).

Virginia Woolf: Bloomsbury novelist who explored the interior lives of women. Played by Nicole Kidman in *The Hours* (2002) and Elizabeth Debicki in *Vita and Virginia* (2018).

Christopher Isherwood: Writer of 20s Berlin who showed us that life was 'a cabaret'. Played by Matt Smith in *Christopher and His Kind* (2011).

Colette: Bisexual French writer and journalist who wrote *Gigi*. Played by Keira Knightley in *Colette* (2018).

ARTISTS

Frida Kahlo: Mexican painter of self-iconography. Played by Salma Hayek in *Frida* (2002).

Salvador Dalí: The poster boy for hyperrealist surrealism. Played by Robert Pattinson in *Little Ashes* (2008).

Dora Carrington: Bloomsbury-adjacent painter of great sensitivity. Played by Emma Thompson in *Carrington* (1995).

Jean-Michel Basquiat: Expressionist street artist and ex-BF of Madonna. Played by Jeffrey Wright in *Basquiat* (1996) and Jeremy Pope in *The Collaboration* (2024).

RuPaul's Drag Race: Iconic Phrases

The queens of *Drag Race* literally changed the way we speak, but some lines are easier to slip into your daily chat than others. Here's some of the best. They aren't ranked. We don't do all that.

"Ya'll wanted a twist, eh?" – Laganja Estranja
USE: When presenting something unexpected.

"Let's get this roast a-cooking." – Farrah Moan
USE: Whenever you're about to start something – especially making dinner.

"I'm ready for another week of me doing mediocre." – Cheryl Hole
USE: On Monday morning.

"Alright public school, calm down." – Trixie Mattel
USE: When posh people get angry.

"Well, you have a blessed night – as will I." – Mistress Isabelle Brooks
USE: To get the last word as you walk away from an argument.

"She is stunosha in this drass-iana." – Denali
USE: When your bestie reveals her gag-worthy outfit.

"I need to get up in this gig, gurl." – Alyssa Edwards
USE: When you're getting ready to go out but are running a teensy bit late.

"No. No. Something else." – Violet Chachki
USE: When you see something that displeases you.

"Very Saint-Tropez." – Jiggly Caliente
USE: For something trying to be super-chic, that isn't.

"Do I have something on my face?" – Pearl
USE: When someone stares you out.

"Calm down, Beyoncé." – Bianca Del Rio
USE: Anytime anyone is acting plucked and grand.

"The level of unprofessionalism . . . far too much." – Latrice Royale
USE: On your friends, colleagues and pets when they're being loud, annoying or disrespectful.

Renaissance Men

The Renaissance began in the 1400s and was the great rebirth of art, inspired by antiquity. Many artists, such as Botticelli, Leonardo da Vinci and Michelangelo, are widely recognised as queer.

The Renaissance was given a homoerotic injection by discoveries of insanely jacked-up ancient statues like *Laocoön and His Sons*, excavated in 1506 and unveiled before Michelangelo's very eyes.

Man (a) Lisa?

When he died, **Leonardo da Vinci** left the *Mona Lisa*, along with other works, to his beautiful long-time male companion who we can all agree was his boyfriend, nicknamed Salaì. The enigmatic portrait is believed by some academics to be of Salaì himself – *Mona Lisa* being an anagram of *Mon Salaì* ('My Salaì' in French). Some art historians suggest that the *Mona Lisa* is a self-portrait of Leonardo in drag. What do you think?

Secrets from the Sistine Chapel

Michelangelo's vast biblical frescos in the Vatican's Sistine Chapel are undoubtedly considered the greatest achievement in the history of art. Guess what? They're very, very gay. Here's why:

1. *The Last Judgement* fresco on the altar wall (1536–1541) isn't just about the damned going to hell and the good going to heaven – it's about giant muscly butts and guys having a gay old time. Look to the far right of Christ and you see a heavenly 'chill out' of naked men kissing.

2. The 20 *ignudi* (naked men) that appear between the famous biblical ceiling scenes in the Sistine Chapel are pretty gay before you even notice the suggestive sheafs of oversized acorns.

3. When Michelangelo's nudes were criticised by the Pope's right-hand man, Biagio da Cesna, the artist got his revenge by painting Biagio as a demon with donkey ears. The year after Michelangelo died, the Church struck back – an artist dubbed Il Braghettone, or 'the breeches-maker', was ordered to paint undies on all the nude figures. Modern restoration has removed many, but not all, of these modesty pants.

Historic TV Moments

LGBTQ+ representation on TV had a slow start, but once it got going – oof, lordy!

1983

Panorama looks at a new medical condition with 12 deaths in the UK: AIDS.

1982

Channel 4's *One in Five* is the first TV show for and about the LGBTQ+ community.

1977

In an episode of *The Jeffersons*, George Jefferson learns that his army buddy Eddie has transitioned. Legendary TV from showrunner Norman Lear.

1988

Two of Us, a BBC Schools drama about two schoolboys falling in love, is nervously aired at . . . 11.30 p.m. Ha ha. Nice try. Thankfully it gets a daytime slot in 1990.

1998

Hayley Cropper, played by Julie Hesmondhalgh, is the first trans character in a soap, ITV's *Coronation Street*.

1999

Queer As Folk airs on Channel 4, ushering in the future of queer programming with its no-holds-barred depiction of LGBTQ+ life in Manchester.

2023

The Last of Us, an HBO zombie show, features a stunning episode about two men falling in love. The core audience of straight young men is . . . conflicted.

2022

Heartstopper on Netflix is a massive hit, proving that queer-focused love stories are *not* niche.

2020

After 16 years of heteronormativity, *Strictly Come Dancing* finally features a same-sex dance pairing, Nicola Adams and Katya Jones.

1959

ITV's play of the week *South* is the first TV show in the UK to address gayness. It also tackles issues surrounding race in the US deep south. Clap emojis all round.

1970

UK audiences watch the first gay TV kiss – between Sir Ian McKellen and James Laurenson in a production of Marlowe's *Edward II* on BBC2.

1973

BBC2 dedicates an entire show, *Open Door*, to trans issues.

1974

Comedy legend Alison Steadman gives us the first lesbian kiss on British TV in the BBC2 drama *Girl*.

2003

The original *Queer Eye* debuts introducing us to Carson Kressley and the Fab Five v1.0.

2009

Vroom, vroom – *RuPaul's Drag Race* screeches onto TV. The most influential LGBTQ+ TV of all time. No contest (there is a contest).

2013

Orange Is the New Black becomes Netflix's first big show – and it's about lesbians and women of colour and bisexual women and trans women and it was fabulous.

2015

Boy Meets Girl is a milestone in trans representation. It's the first UK sitcom to focus on the trans experience, and the first to star a trans actor, Rebecca Root.

2018

With *The Bisexual*, Channel 4 said bye-bye to bi-erasure. Funny, awkward, relatable. Season two, please!

2018

Pose isn't only the first show to feature a cast of trans actors, it's overseen by trans and queer creatives, such as Our Lady J and Janet Mock.

Queerchella

The LGBTQ+ dream festival is happening in on alt Queer Earth-808. Your VIP wristbands are in the post.

From grungy bars to giant arenas and concert halls, queer musicians have been grafting for centuries to create and express themselves. And you're in luck – you get to see the very best, right here and now.

If you had to pick just one day, which would it be?

DAY 1

Main stage

David Bowie • Fever Ray • Janelle Monáe
Little Richard • Kim Petras • La Roux • Soft Cell • The xx

Miley Cyrus • Pet Shop Boys • Scissor Sisters
Samantha Fox • Erasure • Luther Vandross • Rufus Wainwright

Joan Armatrading • Tegan and Sara • Conan Gray
Dusty Springfield • Perfume Genius • Bronski Beat • Holland

Hyper-popped banger pavilion

100 gecs • Charli XCX • Dorian Electra • SOPHIE
Rina Sawayama • Grimes • COBRAH • That Kid • Arca

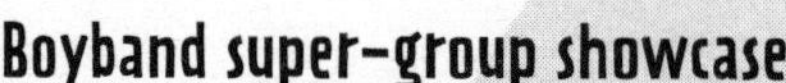

Boyband super-group showcase

Ricky Martin, Menudo • Jon Knight, NKOTB
Carl Fysh, Brother Beyond • Lance Bass, NSYNC
Stephen Gately, Boyzone • Mark Feehliy, Westlife
Duncan James, Blue • George Shelley, Union J

DAY 2

Main stage

Billie Holiday • Lil Nas X • Divine • k.d. lang
Elton John • Frank Ocean • Wendy & Lisa

Queen • St. Vincent • Sister Rosetta Tharpe
The Gossip • Buzzcocks • Hüsker Dü • Kevin Abstract
Skunk Anansie • Shamir • Wee Wee Pole

The B-52's • Joan Jett • Jayne County • Dead Or Alive
Tyler, The Creator • Sia • Tom Robinson
Hunx & His Punx

Euro-vizzy house party

Duncan Laurence • KEiiNO • Katrina
Dana International • Loreen • Gustaph
Lesley Roy • Bilal • Conchita Wurst • Saara Aalto

Alter-ego cabaret tent

Madonna as Dita • Prince as Camille
Janet Jackson as Damita Jo • Lady Gaga as Jo Calderone
Kylie Minogue as Epponnee-Rae

DAY 3

Main stage

The Smiths • Marlene Dietrich • Klaus Nomi
Patrick Wolf • Amanda Lear • King Princess
Alaska Thunderfuck • Ice Spice

Blondie • Blood Orange
Troye Sivan • Kehlani • MUNA • Bloc Party
The Velvet Underground • Orville Peck

George Michael & Wham! • ANHOHNI • Ethel Cain
Joan Baez • Tracy Chapman • Trixie Mattel
dodie • Sam Smith • Arlo Parks • The Singing Nun

Ally support field

SUNMI • Taylor Swift • Mylène Farmer • Harry Styles
Jade Thirlwall • Liza • Cher • Dolly • Bad Bunny
Nile Rodgers • Raffaella Carrà • BTS • Ariana Grande

Composer chill-out

Tchaikovsky • Cole Porter • Ethel Smyth
Lorenz Hart • Handel • Howard Ashman
Schubert • Britten • Greig • Noel Coward
Samuel Barber • Saint Saëns • Mahler • Ned Rorem
Leonard Bernstein • Stephen Sondheim
Ivor Novello • Aaron Copland • John Cage

DAY 4

Main stage

Sylvester • Years & Years • Arthur Russell
Zebra Katz • MNEK • Big Freedia • Fancy
Wendy Carlos

Christine and the Queens • Goldfrapp • Peaches
Hazell Dean • Planningtorock • Patrick Cowley
Fischerspooner

Phoebe Bridgers • Hayley Kiyoko • Justin Vivian Bond
Hercules & Love Affair • Alcazar • BWO
Army Of Lovers • Village People

DJ sets

Larry Levan • Mykki Blanco • Frankie Knuckles
Junior Vasquez • Honey Dijon • Tony De Vit • Larry Tee
Danny Tenaglia • Jonjo Jury • Fat Tony • DJ Ritu
Tracy Young • Readers Wifes • Hannah Holland

Riot Grrrrlies green zone

Bikini Kill • Hole • Sleater-Kinney • Le Tigre
Luscious Jackson • The Breeders • L7
Team Dresch • Huggy Bear • Bratmobile
Veruca Salt • Babes In Toyland

Art Herstory

Horse fairs, fortune-tellers and a freaky doll's house of stocking fillers. A carefully curated collection of trailblazing female talents.

The original horse girl

Rosa Bonheur is one of the most celebrated French artists of the 19th century. Her animal paintings (horses, cows, deer) are not as fashionable as, say, the Impressionists, but they're utterly astonishing. All the while, Bonheur was an unapologetic lesbian trailblazer. She met her lifelong partner in 1836 and dressed in masculine attire with cropped hair, which shocked genteel society. Add to that her hobby of sketching in slaughterhouses and making friends with actual Buffalo Bill of Wild West fame, and you've got a firecracker person as well as painter.

Trans dolls that aren't playing

In the late 1970s, **Greer Lankton** transitioned and the process had a profound and lasting impact on her work: dolls. By the early 1980s, Lankton had become well-known on the New York art scene for her creepy dolls – constructed from pairs of tights, plaster, wire and hair – that were life-sized or Barbie-sized, some beautiful, some grotesque, and many were avatars of the artist herself. Some were wearable and Lankton would disappear inside her own creation.

LGBTQVR

Frustrated by the lack of queer art spaces, **Antonia Forster**, a bisexual engineer and activist from Bristol, decided to learn code and create the world's first virtual LGBTQ+ museum that can be accessed by anyone with a headset and a passion for queer stories and art. Once inside, you can explore 3D scans of real-life objects such as a teddy bear, karaoke mic and a purposefully strewn copy of James Baldwin's *Giovanni's Room*, each accompanied by an audio description.

Obscurity on the cards

If you think of a set of tarot cards, chances are you're thinking of the images painted by **Pamela Colman Smith**, or 'Pixie', a mysterious British artist who was possibly mixed race and almost certainly a lesbian. Smith's 78 beautifully designed cards came out in 1909 and it's estimated that 100 million packs are still in circulation, making her one of the most widely seen artists – yet most of us don't know her name. To identify herself as the artist, she hid her signature, PCS, on every single card. That's not magic, just good sense.

Lost Gay Records

These ground-breaking queer records have been all but forgotten – but deserve another spin.

Lavender Country

Country music is massive in the US, but the southern states that love it aren't famed for their tolerance. That didn't stop pioneering country singer **Patrick Haggerty** from recording an in-your-face queer album, *Lavender Country,* over 50 years ago in 1973. The touching, funny and political songs swing from melancholy drawls to cheery anthems of empowerment.

Olivia Records

In 1973, a group of women set up their own record label, Olivia Records, with the mission to promote the music of women who love women. Co-founder Judy Dlugacz described the endeavour as "ten young radical, feminist lesbians looking to change the world". The record label went on to release 40 albums, including the snappily named compilation *Lesbian Concentrate: A Lesbianthology of Songs and Poems.*

The Dynamic Superiors

Tony Washington should be a household name, yet the first out Black pop star has largely been forgotten. The charismatic singer was the falsetto-blessed frontman of Motown group the Dynamic Superiors. Not only was Tony an early LGBTQ+ Black role model, but his band's banging disco tunes like 'Nobody's Gonna Change Me' and 'Face the Music' absolutely stand the test of time. Surprisingly, Washington's sexuality wasn't supressed by Motown, but embraced.

Closet Man by Dusty Springfield

Great lesbian icon Dusty Springfield bravely came out in 1970, possibly the first massive pop star to do it. Her tender song 'Closet Man', released in 1979, urges a man to come out and it's filled with advice that still resonates today: "There's nothing new at all under the sun, you've got company, you're not the only one, why it's older than religion and quite honestly more fun."

Two songs to take notes to

For queer history you can dance to, stream 'Legendary Children (All of them Queer)' by **Holly Johnson** (1994) and 'Hot Topic' by **Le Tigre** (1999). Johnson runs through his gay faves, including Andy Warhol, Johnnie Ray and Jean Genet in a Vogueish way, while Le Tigre give shout-outs to a who's who of inspirational feminists and activists, from gender-non-conforming stars Vaginal Davis and Billy Tipton to lesbian icons Billie Jean King and Joan Jett.

There's Nowt Queer As Comics

Traditionally the preserve of straight boys, comics and graphic novels have increasingly been embraced by LGBTQ+ readers craving alternate worlds, adventure and escape.

Mother Heartstopper

Alice Oseman is a hero. Not only has she given us *Heartstopper*, the queer coming-of-age story of this age, she has introduced comics to a generation and shown that queer stories have an avid audience, so we should defo pay creators to tell more of them.

Comic's MBE enby

Grant Morrison MBE is one of the UK's most successful comic book authors (*Batman, The X-Men, Doom Patrol, The Invisibles*). They came out as non-binary(ish) in 2020.

Three icons of LGBTQ+ animé

1. *Revolutionary Girl Utena.* Utena doesn't wait for her prince to come. She becomes the prince.
2. *When Marnie Was There.* Bad news! The girl you fancy is your time-travel grandma.
3. *Yuri on Ice.* Superb sports animé that's cringey, sexy, queer. A movie sequel is in production (there is a god).

BL on the DL

In Japan, manga and animé stories where two boys fall in love is a rich and established genre dating back to the 1970s. BL, or Boys' Love, is written by and devoured by a small but devoted mostly female fanbase. BL stories give readers higher-stakes relationships while challenging societal norms. Even conservative South Korea has started to explore BL: check out K-drama *Cherry Blossoms After Winter*.

If you only read one queer comic . . .

. . . make it **Colleen Doran's** gorgeous epic bisexual space opera *A Distant Soil*, which she's been writing since she was 12.

Wonderful Wonder Woman

Wonder Woman made her first appearance in *All Star Comic issue 8* – and since then, she has been bossing it on the page, onscreen and beyond. Years before graphic novels were a thing, feminist author and campaigner **Gloria Steinem** commissioned and paid for the Wonder Woman stories to be collected together and reprinted in book form.

In 1942, *All Star Comics issue 11* asked readers if Wonder Woman should be allowed to join The Justice Society. Readers voted 8–1 in favour, proving that misogyny is learned. Decades later, in 2021, Wonder Woman was given her first girlfriend, Kryptonian Princess Zala Jor-El, proving that she is the bisexual goddess we always knew she was. Sadly, their relationship is set in an alternate universe and Zala is a murderous villain. But, hey, we'll take it.

Bops and Teardrops

There are too many 'essential' queer anthems to name them all, but the best mix-tape ever might include these.

Side A: Bops

B.D. Woman's Blues – Lucille Bogan
Being Boring – Pet Shop Boys
Blind – Hercules and Love Affair ft. Anohni
Closer – Tegan and Sara
Damn, I Wish I Was Your Lover – Sophie B. Hawkins
Girlfriend – Christine and The Queens, ft. Dâm-Funk
I Was Born This Way – Carl Bean
Invisible Light – Scissor Sisters ft. Ian McKellen
Jet Boy, Jet Girl – Elton Motello
Menergy – Patrick Cowley ft. Sylvester
Midnight Sky – Miley Cyrus
Nancy Boy – Placebo
Number One Fan – MUNA
Pynk – Janelle Monáe ft. Grimes
Queer – Garbage
Rush – Troye Sivan
Smalltown Boy – Bronski Beat
Sun Goes Down – Lil Nas X
To The Moon And Back – Fever Ray
Transformation – Nona Hendryx
Wig – The B-52's

Side B: Teardrops

1950 – King Princess
cellophane – FKA twigs
Closer To Fine – Indigo Girls
Eugene – Arlo Parks
Feelings – Hayley Kiyoko
For Today I Am A Boy – Anthony and the Johnsons
go – Cat Burns
Heather – Conan Gray
A House In Nebraska – Ethel Cain
I've Loved You For So Long – The Aces
Ivy – Frank Ocean
Loner – Kali Uchis
Send My Love To John – Rina Sawayama
Sick Of Losing Soulmates – dodie
Sick To My Stomach – Rebecca Black
skyline, be mine – Shura
The Weakness In Me – Joan Armatrading
True Blue – boygenius
we fell in love in october – girl in red
Why Am I Like This? – Orla Gartland
You Have Been Loved – George Michael
Your Ex – Emily Vu

It's a Serve

At the 2022 French Open, there were seven out female players, but no out men. Not one. Zero. Zilch. Love. (No, we do not love.)

The question 'why are there no out gay men playing tennis at an elite level?' is all over the internet, but there are no obvious answers. Whatever the reason, there is no doubt that gay women are serving some blinders. Here are some of the icons.

Gigi Hernandez

When Gigi Hernandez turned professional in 1983, she was Puerto Rico's first professional female in any sport. She came out in 1993, appearing onstage with Martina Navratilova at a gay rights march.

Daria Kasatkina

When Russia's best player, Kasatkina, came out as gay in 2022, it was a massive deal. The country, which has backward anti-LGBTQ+ legislation, needs all the role models for queer youth that it can get.

Billie Jean King

Billie Jean King isn't just a tennis legend, she's a powerhouse advocate for equality. She was the first female athlete to win more than $100,000 in a season (1971). She was one of the first women to coach male professional athletes, and when male former number one player Bobby Riggs challenged her to a 'battle of the sexes' match, she won. In straight sets.

Martina Navratilova

Before the total slayage of the Williams sisters, the Czechia-born Martina Navratilova was the unstoppable record-breaking tennis demon – in fact she has won more tennis titles than any man or woman: 345.

Lisa Raymond

At the top of her game, Lisa Raymond won 11 grand slam titles and still holds the record for most doubles wins of all time – 860, winning more than $10 million.

Renée Richards

Richards underwent gender-confirmation surgery in 1975, and in 1976, applied to play as a woman in the US Open. She refused to take the regulation Barr Body Test, which looks for a particular chromosomal make-up, and was denied permission to enter. Richards sued the United States Tennis Association and won. Her career lasted from 1977 to 1981, after which she coached Martina Navratilova to two Wimbledon wins.

Fascinating Queers: Tove Jansson

The Finnish artist, writer and creator of the Moomins is a national treasure in her homeland and millions of homes around the world too.

The first story Tove Jansson wrote, drew and painted was *The Moomins and the Great Flood* in 1946, followed by *Comet in Moominland* a year later. Jansson created fun characters filled with personality, like Moomintroll, Snork Maiden, Sniff, Snuffkin and Little My and she gave them magical but relatable stories. The floods, comets and blizzards that pepper her stories are as exciting as they are scary – but reading the Moomins comes with a healthy dose of beautiful unspoiled countryside and the wonders of nature. Ahhhhhh.

Despite same-sex relationships not being legal in Finland until 1971, Jansson never tried to hide her preferences. Her first lesbian experience happened while dating a man and she seemed as shocked about it as anyone. "I've fallen madly in love with a woman," she wrote to a friend in 1946. Jansson lived with her partner, Tuulikki Pietilä, for 45 years – Moomins character Too-ticky, introduced in 1958, was based on her. In 1960, Tove and Tuulikki discovered their dream island, Klovharu, and spent their summers there pretty much living the dream Moomin existence.

The Danish kids' book that caused a sensation

One of the first children's books to discuss LGBTQ+ parents also came from Scandinavia. *Jenny Lives with Eric and Martin* by **Susanne Bösche** was a cute picture book about a girl who lives with her dad and his boyfriend. It was published in English in 1983 – but many were not thrilled. A happy gay man raising his daughter? Ban it! And that's what they did. The book was used as a weapon ushering in Section 28, legislation that banned the 'promotion' (mention) of queerness in schools.

Queer Diary . . .

Diaries are important for queer people. They are sometimes the only place we can share our dreams and desires without fear of persecution and ridicule. Even then, some, like Anne Lister, write in code.

Monday
Anne Lister

"I love and only love the fairer sex and thus, beloved by them in turn, my heart revolts from any other love than theirs."

Start the week with the single most important queer diary ever published, that of out-and-proud lesbian landowner Anne Lister, nicknamed 'Gentleman Jack'. Lister (1791–1840) kept a monster of a diary (over 7,000 pages) from the age of 15, chronicling her daily life, which included much seducing of women and searching for a wife.

Tuesday
Joe Orton

"To be young, good-looking, healthy, famous, [. . .] and happy is surely going against nature."

Orton was one of the UK's most anarchic playwrights of the 1960s. He kept a hilarious and frank diary for eight months, at the height of his fame. Quotes like the one above offer a snapshot into what it was to be enthusiastically gay just as it was becoming legal.

Wednesday
Candy Darling

"You must always be yourself, no matter what the price. It is the highest form of morality."

It doesn't get much more heartfelt and bittersweet than this. For some, the Holy Grail of queer memoirs is that of trans superstar Candy Darling, created in the 1960s and 70s. It was first published in 1997, but in such small numbers that copies now sell for around £300. Luckily an e-book is available and affordable. Candy was a delicate creature who never found the love and acceptance that she craved before she died of lymphoma at just 29. Flicking through her diary can be an emotional journey.

Thursday
Andy Warhol

"Jean-Michel [Basquiat] called again from Hawaii. I told him to cut off his ear. He probably will."

Don't worry, he didn't. Artist Andy Warhol knew everyone and he wrote about them all in the most gossipy and dead-pan funny diary that you could ever want to read. He writes about everything else too. Whatever the day is, flap open the book and see what Andy was having for lunch. Who he telephoned. How much his cabs cost.

Friday
Mary MacLane

"I can think of nothing in the world like the utter littleness, the paltriness, the contemptibleness, the degradation, of the woman who [. . .] wears the man's name, who bears the man's children — who plays the virtuous woman . . . "

The words of this Canadian-American feminist writer sting today – so imagine how gobsmacked readers were in 1901. MacLane sold 100,000 copies of her memoir in the first month of publishing, becoming a sensation to young women.

Saturday
Herculine Barbin

"Oh! To live alone, always alone, in the midst of the crowd that surrounds me, without a word of love ever coming to gladden my soul, without a friendly hand reaching out to me!"

In her memoir, French intersex person Barbin (1838–1868) tells the story of her life growing up as a girl in a Catholic orphanage, only to hit puberty and be reclassified as a man. She then went by the name Abel Barbin, but the identity was foreign to her. She kept a journal as a sort of therapy but, sadly, took her own life at age 29. Today, we celebrate Intersex Day of Remembrance on Herculine's birthday, 8th November.

Sunday
Miriam Margolyes

"Not a lot of gay women front up on TV, so I hope I give courage to young dykes to be proud and confident. If you tell the truth – and I always do – you shame the devil."

We must celebrate celebs like Miriam Margolyes because they're so rare. She shows us, more than any other queer celebrity, that we don't have to play nice and sweet to be loved; we just have be ourselves.

Miriam's book, *This Much is True* (2021), is technically a memoir, not a diary, but it's just as eye-wateringly honest. Every word that falls from her mouth has intention: to delight or disturb, challenge or kill us utterly dead.

finally . . .

LGBTQ+ history, society and culture is a specialist subject; not everyone's interested in it. The average person on the street isn't arsed about LGBTQ+ adventures and accomplishments. All too often, the one thing that makes queer people and their allies' ears prick up is the very thing that makes everyone else swipe up, turn off or flip the page.

That's why it's been such an inspirational delight putting this book together; letting every bit of queerness in the world consume me, then plucking out the best bits of this, that and the other that I think everyone would want to know, to create a book that weirdly doesn't exist: a little gay book of everything. As soon as you start looking, there's so much brilliant information about our community. It was nearly impossible to stop dragging stuff to my desktop, filling the Cloud with screenshots or calling up friends to gush about Marlene Dietrich and giraffes.

I think it must be human nature to imagine that the world only got going when we were born, so it comes as a surprise to unearth the shockingly modern and relatable adventures of queer people just like us who lived years, decades, even centuries ago. There's nothing new under the sun and that's humbling, but also comforting. Everything's been done. We might find a new language to explain, celebrate or demonise the LGBTQ+ community, but you can bet that a century from now, the best and worst of us will be discussing exactly the same things just in slightly different ways.

To immerse yourself in queer lives and art is like going to a mental safe space, to feel part of something immense and nourishing. This isn't propaganda; this isn't promotion of a gay agenda – it's just facts. Facts that've been brushed aside because the people in charge thought other things were more important. Things that prop up the status quo. Straight things. Men's things. Gender-conforming things. Bone-dry, dusty, dreary things.

One day, there may be a definitive encyclopaedia of the LGBTQ+ experience, but until then, I hope you enjoyed the whistlestop hits of wildly necessary queer joy.

References

Got Your Number

theguardian.com/world/2022/feb/17/lgbtq-americans-gallup-poll-survey

ons.gov.uk/peoplepopulationandcommunity/culturalidentity/sexuality/articles/sexualorientationageandsexenglandandwales/census2021#how-sexual-orientation-differed-by-age

Call Me By What Name?

plato.stanford.edu/entries/homosexuality/

historians.org/research-and-publications/perspectives-on-history/may-2017/tracing-terminology-researching-early-uses-of-cisgender

queerty.com/15-general-population-may-now-identify-heteroflexible-study-finds-20200131

espu.org/members/documents/383-espu-spu-consensus-statement-2020-management-of-differences-of-sex-development-dsd

ncbi.nlm.nih.gov/pmc/articles/PMC1449332/

Biology Lesson

nytimes.com/2019/08/29/science/gay-gene-sex.html

science.org/doi/full/10.1126/science.aat7693

theguardian.com/science/2005/may/12/thisweeksciencequestions1

independent.co.uk/news/science/sense-of-smell-is-linked-to-sexual-orientation-study-reveals-490147.html

edition.cnn.com/2000/HEALTH/03/29/gay.fingers/

nbcnews.com/feature/nbc-out/men-older-brothers-are-more-likely-be-gay-study-suggests-n1165201

pnas.org/content/115/2/234

ncbi.nlm.nih.gov/pmc/articles/PMC3402034/

bbc.co.uk/news/health-45887691

yougov.co.uk/topics/politics/trackers/what-determines-sexuality-according-to-brits?crossBreak=65plus

Q. How Many Sexes?

A. It's Complicated

scientificamerican.com/article/q-a-mixed-sex-biology/

theglobeandmail.com/opinion/think-gender-comes-down-to-x-and-y-chromosomes-think-again/article24811543/

joshuakennon.com/the-six-common-biological-sexes-in-humans/

novonordiskfonden.dk/en/news/more-women-than-expected-are-genetically-men/

news-medical.net/health/What-is-Superman-Syndrome.aspx

amnesty.org/en/latest/news/2018/10/its-intersex-awareness-day-here-are-5-myths-we-need-to-shatter/

pubmed.ncbi.nlm.nih.gov/12476264/

ncbi.nlm.nih.gov/books/NBK557435/

nhs.uk/conditions/androgen-insensitivity-syndrome/

https://www.theguardian.com/film/2023/jun/28/intersex-documentary-every-body-what-does-it-mean

https://urldefense.com/v3/__https://www.gov.uk/government/news/government-calls-for-evidence-on-people-who-have-variations-in-sex-characteristics__;!!F0Stn7g!F0CJGaSox4n2RLkUSJ_s9wD8u0F3xYiUDLw3P28mnxW42YhUHKFqvkl5ZOkfG0_FJSMzNaDOFuQq-N8IfqSXTejj4PaCaZTofA$

You Filthy Animal

imperial.ac.uk/news/190987/scientists-explore-evolution-animal-homosexuality/

cambridge.org/core/journals/polar-record/article/abs/dr-george-murray-levick-18761956-unpublished-notes-on-the-sexual-habits-of-the-adelie-penguin/8647660D29AD9660C9C16623638C9116

blogs.scientificamerican.com/observations/why-is-same-sex-sexual-behavior-so-common-in-animals/

dw.com/en/10-animal-species-that-show-how-being-gay-is-natural/g-39934832

discoverwildlife.com/animal-facts/can-animals-be-gay/

nytimes.com/2010/04/04/magazine/04animals-t.html

Homophobia: The Dark Side of the Rainbow

thepinknews.com/2022/08/15/anti-lgbtq-hate-crime-police-uk/

researchbriefings.files.parliament.uk/documents/CBP-8537/CBP-8537.pdf

theguardian.com/society/2022/oct/17/young-lgbtq-people-more-than-twice-as-likely-to-experience-hate-speech-online

theguardian.com/society/2019/sep/11/homophobic-hate-charges-reports

Age of Consent Around the World

features.hrw.org/features/features/lgbt_laws/

humandignitytrust.org/lgbt-the-law/map-of-criminalisation/

equaldex.com/issue/age-of-consent

ourworldindata.org/grapher/age-of-consent-for-same-sex-partners-unequal-to-heterosexual-partners

statista.com/statistics/1227390/number-of-countries-that-criminalize-homosexuality/

sexualalpha.com/age-of-consent-by-country/

database.ilga.org/criminalisation-consensual-same-sex-sexual-acts

humandignitytrust.org/lgbt-the-law/map-of-criminalisation/?type_filter_submitted=&type_filter%5B%5D=crim_sex_men

A-Z of Queer Spaces
washingtonpost.com/news/wonk/wp/2015/05/27/the-countries-where-gay-men-are-the-happiest/

Labelling the Past
academic.oup.com/jcb/article/28/3/580/2548295

OG Queers
Translation of Sappho's Fragment 31 by Bliss Carson, 1907 (p. 81)

Worldwide Pride
ipsos.com/sites/default/files/ct/news/documents/2023-05/Ipsos%20LGBT%2B%20Pride%202023%20Global%20Survey%20Report%20-%20rev.pdf

investmentmonitor.ai/features/largest-cities-uk-investment-strengths/

ons.gov.uk/peoplepopulationandcommunity/culturalidentity/sexuality/articles/sexualorientationageandsexenglandandwales/census2021#how-sexual-orientation-differed-by-age

humandignitytrust.org/news/angola-joins-growing-list-of-countries-eradicating-out-dated-sexual-offences-laws/

humandignitytrust.org/news/high-court-decision-huge-win-for-human-rights-of-lgbt-people-in-botswana-and-beyond/

humandignitytrust.org/news/mozambique-decriminalises-same-sex-sexual-conduct-between-consenting-adults/

hrw.org/news/2023/05/30/ugandas-president-signs-repressive-anti-lgbt-law

theweek.com/news/world-news/us/957029/one-in-20-americans-under-30-identifies-as-nonbinary

pewresearch.org/social-trends/2022/06/07/the-experiences-challenges-and-hopes-of-transgender-and-nonbinary-u-s-adults/

washingtonpost.com/lifestyle/2022/10/14/anti-trans-bills/

Colonialism and LGBTQ+ Freedoms
centaur.reading.ac.uk/80592/1/British%20Colonialism%20and%20the%20Criminalization%20of%20Homosexuality-Final%20Revision.pdf

About the Creators

Malcolm Mackenzie is an award-winning author, editor, journalist, with an encyclopaedic knowledge of pop culture. He describes his younger self as painfully bullyable, but somehow never ashamed, no easy task for a kid at Catholic school during the AIDS crisis on an island with regressive anti-LGBTQ+ laws. He credits Channel 4 – which introduced him to pioneering disruptors Leigh Bowery, Derek Jarman, Julian Clary, Lea DeLaria and RuPaul – with opening a portal to an exciting queer alternative. Since those days stuck on the rock, he's interviewed gay icons like Lady Gaga, Taylor Swift, Kylie Minogue, Harry Styles and Dolly Parton as well as queer artists such as John Waters, Todd Haynes, Billy Porter, Anohni and Miley Cyrus. His most prized possession is a birthday card from Quentin Crisp.

Emily A. Foster is a queer, autistic illustrator who creates inclusive and joyful artwork. Her work celebrates diversity and aims to create a world everyone can recognise themselves in.